Y8   + 48!

School Violence

by Peggy J. Parks

Current Issues

ReferencePoint
Press™

San Diego, CA

ReferencePoint
Press™

© 2009 ReferencePoint Press, Inc.

For more information, contact:
ReferencePoint Press, Inc.
PO Box 27779
San Diego, CA 92198
www. ReferencePointPress.com

Picture credits:
Maury Aaseng: 32–35, 49–52, 65–67, 80–83
AP Images: 11, 14

Parks, Peggy J., 1951–
  School violence / by Peggy J. Parks.
    p. cm.—(Compact research series)
  Includes bibliographical references and index.
  ISBN-13: 978-1-60152-057-9 (hardback)
  ISBN-10: 1-60152-057-3 (hardback)
  1. School violence—United States—Juvenile literature. I. Title.
  LB3013.32.P37 2008
  371.7'82—dc22   2008018372

Contents

Foreword

66Where is the knowledge we have lost in information?99

—"The Rock," T.S. Eliot.

As modern civilization continues to evolve, its ability to create, store, distribute, and access information expands exponentially. The explosion of information from all media continues to increase at a phenomenal rate. By 2020 some experts predict the worldwide information base will double every 73 days. While access to diverse sources of information and perspectives is paramount to any democratic society, information alone cannot help people gain knowledge and understanding. Information must be organized and presented clearly and succinctly in order to be understood. The challenge in the digital age becomes not the creation of information, but how best to sort, organize, enhance, and present information.

ReferencePoint Press developed the *Compact Research* series with this challenge of the information age in mind. More than any other subject area today, researching current issues can yield vast, diverse, and unqualified information that can be intimidating and overwhelming for even the most advanced and motivated researcher. The *Compact Research* series offers a compact, relevant, intelligent, and conveniently organized collection of information covering a variety of current topics ranging from illegal immigration and methamphetamine to diseases such as anorexia and meningitis.

The series focuses on three types of information: objective single-author narratives, opinion-based primary source quotations, and facts and statistics. The clearly written objective narratives provide context and reliable background information. Primary source quotes are carefully selected and cited, exposing the reader to differing points of view. And facts and statistics sections aid the reader in evaluating perspectives. Presenting these key types of information creates a richer, more balanced learning experience.

For better understanding and convenience, the series enhances information by organizing it into narrower topics and adding design features that make it easy for a reader to identify desired content. For example, in *Compact Research: Illegal Immigration*, a chapter covering the economic impact of illegal immigration has an objective narrative explaining the various ways the economy is impacted, a balanced section of numerous primary source quotes on the topic, followed by facts and full-color illustrations to encourage evaluation of contrasting perspectives.

The ancient Roman philosopher Lucius Annaeus Seneca wrote, "It is quality rather than quantity that matters." More than just a collection of content, the *Compact Research* series is simply committed to creating, finding, organizing, and presenting the most relevant and appropriate amount of information on a current topic in a user-friendly style that invites, intrigues, and fosters understanding.

School Violence at a Glance

Prevalence

Nearly 80 percent of schools in the United States experienced one or more violent crime incidents during the 2005–2006 school year; 17 percent had one or more serious violent incidents.

Causes

Many different factors contribute to school violence, including emotional instability, family problems, alcohol and/or drugs, the ease of obtaining weapons, and gang involvement.

Bullying

Some acts of school violence are caused by retaliation against bullying. The Centers for Disease Control and Prevention (CDC) reports that 30 percent of sixth to tenth graders have either been a bully, a victim of bullying, or both.

Incident Reporting by Schools

Studies by private research firms have shown that many assaults and other violent acts in schools are not reported to law enforcement, which affects the accuracy of national statistics.

School Shootings

According to the CDC, less than 1 percent of all youth homicides occur at school.

Keeping Students Safe

Many schools have installed metal detectors, surveillance cameras, and random search programs and use lockdowns when any suspicious activity occurs inside or near a school.

Overview

A ccording to the Bureau of Justice Statistics, 78 percent of schools in the United States experienced one or more violent incidents of crime during the 2005–2006 school year, and 17 percent experienced one or more serious violent incidents. By far, school shootings receive the greatest amount of attention from the news media; yet as horrifying as they are, these acts of violence are actually quite uncommon. The news media are often accused of blowing the events out of proportion and unnecessarily frightening the public. University of Virginia psychologist Dewey Cornell explains:

> We have over 2,000 children murdered each year in the U.S. Only about a dozen or so are murdered at school. If the media gave equal attention to every shooting in a restaurant, we would soon start fearing restaurants. We

would talk about "restaurant violence." We would talk about "restaurant shooters." And unfortunately, some deranged and troubled individuals would be inspired to carry out restaurant shootings.[1]

Teachers, as well as students, are frequent victims of school violence. This is a problem in many cities, one of which is Cleveland, Ohio. During the 2006–2007 school year, 281 assaults and 215 threats were reportedly made against teachers in Cleveland district schools. In January 2008 teacher James Cappetto was viciously attacked by students at Cleveland's South High School. He noticed a fight going on and moved in to break it up. While trying to shield a football player beneath him, Cappetto was beaten on the head and back, possibly with brass knuckles. The attack left him with a

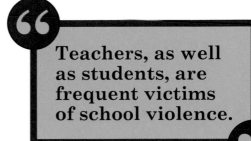

Teachers, as well as students, are frequent victims of school violence.

fractured skull and 3 broken vertebrae in his neck. Another teacher in the Cleveland school district, Marylou Prescott, has also encountered violence, which she says has a detrimental effect on educators' ability to help students. She explains: "For some reason these students view life as having no purpose. They don't see what a better life education will bring to them. And as a result, their actions are scaring teachers. And that prevents teachers from providing any education at all."[2]

What Are the Causes of School Violence?

Just as many different types of school violence exist, a number of different factors can contribute to it. One of the most common catalysts for violent acts in schools is bullying and harassment by classmates. According to Laurence Miller, a clinical and forensic psychologist, this sort of victimization can lead to damaged self-esteem, anxiety and panic attacks, depression, and suicidal thoughts. Students who are severely, repeatedly bullied often do not want to go to school, suffer from impaired academic performance, and become increasingly lonely and isolated.

The Centers for Disease Control and Prevention (CDC) reports that an estimated 30 percent of sixth to tenth graders in the United States have either been a bully, a target of bullying, or both. A 2007 report by the National Center for Education Statistics showed that in 2005, 28 percent of students aged 12 to 18 reported having been bullied at school during the previous 6 months; 11 percent had been bullied once or twice a week, and 8 percent had been bullied almost daily. Miller says that bullying in schools is more common than people may know, as he explains:

> The kinds of intimidation and harassment that would get an employee fired at almost any job is routinely tolerated by school authorities when it occurs between students. In virtually every case of school violence studied, the perpetrators had been harassed or persecuted in some way by other students and their efforts to have their cases resolved by school authorities were rebuffed or ignored. Of course, a far greater number of bullied students suffer in silence without seeking to redress their injustice with a greater atrocity.[3]

Fifteen-year-old Charles Andrew Williams was one who "suffered in silence" when he was relentlessly bullied at his Santee, California, high school. He was the victim of repeated and unprovoked attacks, as students burned cigarette lighters and held the hot metal against his neck, or walked up to him and punched him in the face—yet Williams told no one. Then in March 2001 he decided to get even. He removed his father's gun from a cabinet, took it to school, and went on a shooting spree. By the time police apprehended him, 2 students were dead and 13 others were wounded.

The reality, though, is that only a tiny fraction of students who are bullied by classmates actually kill others—and those who do likely have problems that go far beyond bullying. Most suffer from severe mental health problems and/or emotional issues as well as family problems, as crisis counselor Marleen Wong explains: "A lot of the school shooters have suffered a recent loss, or feel they have suffered a failure; they didn't have a positive connection with anyone inside their families or outside their families."[4]

School Violence and Gangs

A disturbing amount of the violence in America's schools is related to gangs. According to the U.S. Department of Justice, about 30,000 gangs

On April 16, 2007, Virginia Polytechnic Institute and State University in Blacksburg, Virginia, was the site of America's deadliest school shooting. The shooter, Seung-Hui Cho, killed 32 people before turning the gun on himself. This shooting victim was rescued by law enforcement officers and has since recovered from his wounds.

and 800,000 gang members are active in the United States. A 2007 report by the National Center for Education Statistics showed that in 2005, 24 percent of students surveyed said that gangs were at their school, up from 21 percent in 2003. Cities all over the country struggle with gang problems in schools, such as in Baltimore, Maryland. Because of a citywide reshaping of high schools, rival gangs now often share the same building, and this has led to ongoing violent disputes. When the principal of Homeland Security Academy in West Baltimore implemented school uniforms of royal blue polo shirts and khaki pants, gang-related fights started breaking out immediately. Blue is the color associated with the Crips gang, while members of the rival Bloods gang wear red. Student Brittany Harris explains why this led to a clash of gangs: "It's all because of this color. When they [Bloods] see you with this color, they try to fight you."[5]

> A disturbing amount of the violence in America's schools is related to gangs.

Los Angeles is another city that constantly struggles with gang violence, including in and around schools. In July 2006, 17-year-old Agustin Contreras was shot and killed by gang members in his school's parking lot. His younger brother said that two young men approached him and told him to hand over the diamond-studded cross that he had around his neck. One grabbed for the chain and yelled out the name of a local gang, and as Agustin tried to help his brother, he was fatally shot. Los Angeles police chief William Bratton expresses how serious a problem gang-related violence is in his city: "Every day we've got significant violence in our schools, and it is created and controlled by gangs."[6]

Should Violent Entertainment Be Blamed for School Violence?

After a school shooting or other act of violence, it is not uncommon for people to look for someone or something to blame. Victims, their families, school administrators, and law enforcement begin asking questions about what may have contributed to the violence—and violent entertainment is sometimes blamed, at least in part, for real-life violent acts. This is a highly controversial issue, as many people insist that no source of entertainment can possibly influence someone to shoot up a school or commit other violent crimes. Jason Della Rocca, executive director of the International Game Developers Association, explains his views: "It's so sad. These massacre chasers—they're worse than ambulance chasers—they're waiting for these things to happen so they can jump on their soapbox."[7]

According to the National Institute on Media and the Family, by the time a child is 18 years old, he or she will have witnessed 200,000 acts of violence on television, including 40,000 murders. Those who attribute violence to violent entertainment express the most concern about violent video games, especially "first-person shooter" games. Unlike movies and TV shows, which are passive forms of entertainment, a player holding the joystick is in control of maiming and killing the game's characters. This, some people claim, can have a detrimental effect on young people by desensitizing them to violent acts and possibly inciting them to act violently themselves. After the April 2007 shooting deaths of 32 people at Virginia Tech University, Florida attorney Jack Thompson lashed out at the developers of *Counter-Strike*, a video game that real-life shooter Seung-Hui Cho had reportedly played often. "This is not rocket science," Thompson says. "When a kid who has never killed anyone in his life goes on a rampage and looks like the Terminator, he's a video gamer."[8]

Violence 101

In April 1999 students Eric Harris and Dylan Klebold committed an act of violence that shocked and stunned people around the world. Armed with an arsenal of weapons, they went on a deadly shooting spree at Columbine High School in Littleton, Colorado, killing 12 students, one teacher, and themselves, and leaving more than 20 others injured. Yet as tragic as the massacre was, if it had gone the way Harris and Klebold had origi-nally planned, there could have been hundreds of deaths. Their plan was to blow up the school cafeteria during lunch period, when it was most crowded, and then shoot students as they tried to escape. This was foiled when the bomb they planted failed to go off, so the gunmen started shooting people they encountered in the cafeteria, hallways, classrooms, and the library.

> " As they were plotting their murderous rampage, Harris and Klebold found step-by-step instructions for building bombs on the Internet. "

Subsequent investigations uncovered some shocking findings: As they were plotting their murderous rampage, Harris and Klebold found step-by-step instructions for building bombs on the Internet. Once they had downloaded the information, Harris posted explicit instructions on his own Web site to help other would-be bombers. He also wrote violent

Los Angeles police monitor the front entrance of this high school after a gang-related brawl broke out between students. Gang membership in Los Angeles schools has become a serious problem.

rhetoric on the site, saying that his desire was to "blow up and shoot everything I can. Feel no remorse, no sense of shame . . . I don't care if I live or die in the shootout, all I want to do is kill and injure as many of you [expletive] as I can." Harris boasted that he and a friend, code-named "VoDka" (Klebold), had made four pipe bombs and had detonated one, which he described on the site as "heart-pounding gut-wrenching brain-twitching ground-moving insanely cool!"[9]

Less than a month after the Columbine massacre, four eighth graders from Wimberley, Texas, were arrested after they were overheard plotting to kill students and teachers by blowing up Danforth Junior High School. Authorities who searched their homes said they found explosive devices and gunpowder, as well as bomb-building instructions that were downloaded from the Internet. Fortunately, their plot was discovered before they could act on it, and they were charged with conspiracy to manufacture explosives and commit murder and arson.

Today a wealth of information is available on the Internet that can aid students in committing violent acts. According to Safer Child, among the sites that kids can access are those with information about bombs, guns, hate groups, dangerous products, and destructive lifestyles. Numerous Web sites also offer guns, ammunition, and firearm supplies for sale. An April 2007 article in the *Economist* stated that the AK-47 assault weapon could be purchased online for $379.99, and a wide variety of other weapons are also offered for sale online.

Because of how destructive these Web sites can be, many people do not understand why they are still online and believe they should be outlawed. In the United States, however, information on the Internet cannot be censored, as it is protected under the First Amendment, which states: "Congress shall make no law . . . abridging the freedom of speech."

Do Alcohol and Drugs Contribute to School Violence?

According to the FBI, school violence offenders' use of drugs and alcohol is minimal. From 2000 to 2004, the agency reports that 589,534 criminal offenses occurred in U.S. schools; offenders suspected of using drugs totaled 32,366, while offenders suspected of using alcohol totaled 5,844. But in some schools drugs and alcohol play a more significant role in school violence. In North Carolina, for instance, 11,013 acts of violence occurred during the 2006–2007 school year; drugs were involved in 4,339 of the incidents and alcohol was involved in 1,081—nearly 50 percent of the total. According to the Department of Education's Linda Langford, alcohol plays a significant role in crime on college campuses. She explains: "One researcher estimates that between 50 and 80 percent of violence on campus is alcohol-related, and about 50 percent of campus sexual assaults are associated with drinking as well."[10] Langford adds that campus vicinities typically have a number of liquor stores and bars nearby, and research shows that areas with greater availability of alcohol typically have higher levels of crime.

Some studies have linked antidepressants and other prescription drugs with violent behaviors, and the U.S. Food and Drug Administration warns that violence and suicide are possible side effects of taking the drugs. Stephen P. Kazmierczak, who on February 14, 2008, killed five students and himself at Northern Illinois University, was taking a mixture of antianxiety drugs as well as a sleeping aid. Some have speculated that the combination of drugs may have contributed to Kazmierczak's violent actions, although this was never proved.

What Is the Aftermath of School Violence?

Brian Anderson cringes whenever he hears the sound of a helicopter. Anne Marie Hocchalter is paralyzed and confined to a wheelchair. Steve Cobenais has a traumatic brain injury and suffers from epileptic seizures. Chon Gai'la is haunted by violent nightmares. Chris Reynolds wonders if he could possibly have stopped a shooting from happening. Andrea Barone still has flashbacks of the crack of gunfire and a killer wearing a black coat. Whether the effects of school violence are physical or psychological, they are devastating to all those who are left behind. As school violence documentary producer Rebecca Cressman explains, "It's not just about taking safety precautions at school. It's not just about preventing death. It's about preserving a young person's confidence and his world. Once they've gone through that trauma event, it reverberates in his life for decades to come."[11]

> " Some psychologists believe that this deep emotional trauma is even more severe than what soldiers suffer through war experiences. "

Some psychologists believe that this deep emotional trauma is even more severe than what soldiers suffer through war experiences. Florida psychologist Charles R. Figley explains: "It's much, much worse. You're not trained, you're not prepared. You can become a prisoner to that experience."[12]

Should Teachers Be Armed?

As uncommon as school shootings are, no one knows when one might happen—and because of that, some people advocate taking extreme measures to prevent them. One proposed solution they offer is to allow teachers and administrators to carry weapons on campus and in classrooms. Currently, 38 states and the District of Columbia have laws that specifically ban all guns at schools, and 16 of those prohibit guns in colleges and universities. Many administrators, teachers' organizations, and law enforcement agencies favor such laws, but more and more people are speaking out, saying that educators should be able to carry concealed weapons to protect themselves and their students against potential violence. Clark Aposhian, who runs a gun training course for teachers, offers his thoughts: "We'll never know if in Baley or Pennsylvania or Red Lake, Minn., if a firearm discreetly carried by a teacher or an administrator or custodian would have stopped these shootings, if it would have saved any lives at all. However, we can tell you with absolute certainty what happened when no firearms were carried by teachers."[13]

How Schools Protect Students

Schools throughout the United States have implemented various programs and procedures to keep students safe. Cornell believes that this should be done on a case-by-case basis, depending on what makes the most sense at a particular school. "Some schools need more security than others," he says. "Some schools need locked doors because the neighborhood is dangerous. We cannot generalize to all schools because of the unusual, extreme cases. We need to look at the needs of each school, factually and objectively and see what security needs that school has."[14] One precautionary measure that many schools use when suspicious activity occurs inside or near a school is the lockdown. Once a lockdown is ordered by law enforcement, all the school's doors are closed and locked, and no one is allowed to enter or leave the building until it has been searched and is declared safe. This happened in February 2008, when a teenage girl at a Pasadena, California, high school told a teacher that her boyfriend was coming to shoot her. Police were notified and the school was locked down for the entire day as officers searched every room and every person. No gun was found, but the young man was arrested and taken to jail for allegations of gun possession and for making criminal threats.

Some schools use metal detectors that everyone must walk through before entering the building, as well as surveillance cameras that constantly monitor activity in hallways and other areas. Random search programs have been implemented in many schools, whereby students line up and security guards pick students at random and check them for weapons using scanning wands. Also, more and more schools are partnering with local law enforcement and have armed police officers patrolling the halls during the school day.

Can School Violence Be Stopped?

Law enforcement officials, security consultants, educators, and school administrators are constantly looking for ways to prevent violent acts in schools and to stop them quickly if they do happen. But this is a daunting task—the country has more than 120,000 public and private schools, and experts say that it is virtually impossible to anticipate every potential act of violence. They say, however, that a crucial step toward preventing school violence is awareness that it is always a possibility.

According to Cornell, one of the most successful ways of deterring violence in schools is educating students about the harmful effects of bullying. He cites more than 200 studies on school-based violence prevention and says that bullying education programs have been shown to reduce fighting and other violence by as much as 50 percent. One of these programs, which has become part of the curriculum in high schools throughout Connecticut, is known as "Names Can Really Hurt Us," or "Names" for short. The program utilizes specially trained teachers and student volunteers, as well as facilitators from the Anti-Defamation League, who educate students about how devastating bullying, name-calling, and bigotry can be. At the end of each segment, participants are invited to get up and speak during an open-mike session. On one particular occasion, a teenage boy stood up, took the microphone, and spoke candidly—and his words were indicative of how the program had affected him emotionally. "I just want to say I'm up here talking for me and my friends," he said. "You all know us, right? Yeah. I've probably picked on most of you. And if any of us made fun of you, I'm here to tell you we're sorry. It wasn't cool. We're really sorry. Peace."[15]

How Widespread Is School Violence?

Violence is an unfortunate fact of life most everywhere. But when violence takes place at school, it is considered especially tragic because schools are places where young people should always feel safe. Some insist that the problem of school violence is exaggerated by the media, such as with massive publicity about school shootings. But for anyone whose life has been touched by violence, it does not matter whether it is common or rare—all that matters is the scars it leaves behind. Laura Standley, who lived through a school shooting in Philadelphia, shares her thoughts: "Unfortunately, no student can walk into a class building without knowing that it could happen here too. That is an awful thing to have occupying the back of your mind. That inherent knowledge every student now possesses really makes attending classes a lot less desirable now, doesn't it?"[16]

"He Just Fires Right into the Audience"

On April 16, 2007, Virginia Polytechnic Institute and State University in Blacksburg, Virginia, was the site of America's deadliest school shooting. It began at 7:15 A.M., when Seung-Hui Cho, a 23-year-old Virginia Tech senior, shot and killed 2 students in the West Ambler Johnston Hall dormitory. Just over 2 hours later, armed with 2 handguns, Cho moved over to Norris Hall, where classes were being held, and continued his shooting spree. According to witnesses, the gunman was silent and showed no emotion as he moved through the building, firing at people in hallways and classrooms. By the time the bloody rampage was over, 28 students (including Cho) and 5 faculty members were dead, and more than 24 others were injured.

Less than a year later, Northern Illinois University in DeKalb was the scene of another school shooting. On the afternoon of Valentine's Day 2008, former student Stephen P. Kazmierczak entered the rear stage door of a room where a class was under way. Dressed all in black and wielding a shotgun and three handguns, Kazmierczak walked onto the stage and began firing. "He just fires right into the audience," says student John Giovanni. "He didn't say a word. It didn't look like he was aiming directly at someone. I think he was trying to hit as many people as he could."[17] Panic erupted as students dropped to the floor in an attempt to avoid the spray of bullets, while others crawled, ran, or shoved their way toward the doors. In a matter of seconds, 5 people were dead and 16 others were wounded. Then, still standing on the stage, Kazmierczak shot himself to death.

> On April 16, 2007, Virginia Polytechnic Institute and State University in Blacksburg, Virginia, was the site of America's deadliest school shooting.

The bloody rampage in DeKalb was the fifth shooting of an especially violent week in American schools. On February 7, 2008, William

Michael Layne entered Notre Dame Elementary School in Portsmouth, Ohio, walked into his ex-wife's classroom, fired a gun in the air, and then stabbed her in front of her fifth-grade class. On February 8, nursing student Latina Williams shot and killed 2 classmates and herself at a technical college in Baton Rouge, Louisiana. On February 11, 17-year-old Corneilous Cheers, a student from Mitchell High School in Memphis, shot and critically injured a classmate. On February 13, Brandon McInerney shot and killed a classmate at an Oxnard, California, high school.

How Often Do School Shootings Happen?

According to a report by ABC News, 323 students died in documented school shootings between 1992 and 2007, making it the largest cause of violent school-related deaths. Daniel Gross, who founded the antiviolence group PAX after his brother was shot and critically wounded, claims that this is an urgent matter that needs to be taken seriously. "Every day there is a new story about children shooting other children, bringing guns to school or worse, actually killing someone," he says. "What does it take before we stop as a nation and try to address an issue that can affect any of us at any moment?"[18]

As tragic as school shootings are, however, they are much more rare than people may realize. Although homicide is the second most common cause of death among children 5 to 18 years old, the Centers for Disease Control and Prevention reports that less than 1 percent of all youth homicides occur at school. In 2006, for instance, 2,700 young people under the age of 22 were killed by firearms, but during the 2005–2006 school year, just 15 of those shooting deaths happened in school. "Schools remain safe places,"[19] says CDC behavioral scientist Jeff Hall. A 2007 CDC study, for which Hall was the lead author, showed that between 1999 and 2006, 116 students were killed at school, with 65 percent of those deaths the result of shootings. But when compared with the estimated 70 million students who are enrolled in American schools and colleges, the number of school-related shooting deaths as a percentage is very low.

A Catastrophic Fire

Because of extensive publicity, including the immediacy of news on the Web, many are under the impression that school violence is a relatively new occurrence. As Laurence Miller writes, "School violence is not really back in the news because it never left."[20] It is also commonly believed that the most violent acts at schools involve shootings. And while that is often true, the worst school massacre in U.S. history occurred more than 50 years ago—and it was the not the result of guns, but a disastrous fire.

On the afternoon of December 1, 1958, a fire broke out in the basement of Our Lady of the Angels Catholic school in Chicago. The school had just one fire escape, no smoke detectors or sprinklers, and no alarm connected to the fire department. As terrified children and nuns scrambled to escape, flames raced through the 2-story building, and smoke and toxic gases filled the air. By the time firefighters had the fire under control, the disaster had claimed the lives of 92 children and 3 nuns and left more than 100 others injured.

Four years later, in a meeting with polygraph expert John Reid, a boy who had been a fifth grader at the time of the fire confessed that he had started it. The boy stated:

> I asked my teacher if I could be excused and went to the
> washroom. After coming from the washroom I went to the
> chapel to see if anyone was in there. Then from the chapel
> I went back to this here can like janitors have, it was made
> out of cardboard like and had steel rims on it and I didn't
> see anybody no place and I used three matches and I lit
> the thing and I ran back upstairs to my room.[21]

The boy's confession was supported by details about the fire's origin that had not been relayed to the public and that only the arsonist could have known. In spite of the confession, however, and Reid's strong belief that the boy was guilty, family court judge Alfred J. Cilella refused to hold him accountable. To this day, the cause of the fire is officially listed as undetermined.

What Types of School Violence Are Most Common?

School-related violence can involve everything from playground beatings to robbery and assault. According to the FBI's October 2007 "Crime in Schools and Colleges" report, from 2000 to 2004 there were more than 181,000 arrests made due to crime in schools, including nearly 16,000 arrests for simple and aggravated assault. The FBI also says that while the greatest number of school-related homicides are committed with guns, nonfatal violent crimes are more often committed with other weapons. For instance, over the 5-year period covered in the report, there were 10,970 school-related incidents involving knives or other cutting instruments, compared with 3,461 incidents that involved a firearm.

Schools in Baltimore, Maryland, have an ongoing struggle with violence in hallways, classrooms, and outside on school grounds. During the first 2 months of the 2006–2007 school year, incidents leading to arrests by school police were up 26 percent in the city compared with the previous year. Students often use their cell phone cameras to record school fights and then post the videoclips online, one of which showed students at Baltimore's Mergenthaler Vocational-Technical High School trying to throw a girl out of a window. In October 2007 a 15-year-old girl at Baltimore's Forest Park High School stabbed a 17-year-old girl in the chest after the older girl threw chalk at her, and later that month a male student set a girl's hair on fire.

> " According to a report by ABC News, 323 students died in documented school shootings between 1992 and 2007, making it the largest cause of violent school-related deaths. "

Bullying remains one of the most serious problems in schools throughout the United States. Many of California's public schools are plagued with problems of bullying and harassment based on sexual orientation, ethnicity, religion, or disability. Lance Chih, a graduate of Folsom High School in Folsom, California, says he was the constant victim of bullying. He explains: "Three years ago, I experienced a series of hate crimes for being gay—starting with a death threat, moving on to a physical attack, and ending with sexual harassment in front of a teacher by two male students."[22] In February 2008, 14-year-old Adrian Ulm, who had been the victim of verbal abuse for two years, was brutally beaten at a school bus stop in Denver while a dozen other students stood by and watched. Ulm's collarbone was broken in the beating and his face was cut and badly bruised. His attacker was expelled from school, but Ulm's friends told Ulm that he could expect an even worse beating when the boy returned.

How Accurate Are School Violence Statistics?

According to the National Center for Education Statistics, students aged 12 to 18 were victims of about 1.5 million nonfatal crimes at school during 2005. A separate report showed that 628,000 students aged 12 to 18 were victims of some type of violent crime in schools during 2005, which was nearly equal to the number of violent crime victims away from school. Still, though, government reports show that violence in schools has markedly decreased since the early 1990s, even by as much as half.

Some, however, question those findings, saying that the actual number of crime victims could be significantly higher. The Cleveland firm National School Safety and Security Services states that there are "countless documented examples of serious school crime and serious incident underreporting, nonreporting, and delayed reporting across the United States."[23] The organization cites multiple examples of this happening, such as in January 2008 when a state-appointed school safety monitor reported that two incidents at an elementary school were not reported to police. One of the incidents involved a student who was caught at school with a knife, and in the other incident a student attempted to stab a classmate with scissors. This inaccuracy has been partly blamed on a provision of the No Child Left Behind Act, which requires states to label violent schools as "persistently dangerous." According to a December 2007 article in the *Baltimore Sun*, teachers and administrators throughout the country say they have been discouraged from reporting violent incidents in order to avoid the negative designation.

> While the greatest number of school-related homicides are committed with guns, nonfatal violent crimes are more often committed with other weapons.

Underreporting or inconsistent reporting of violent acts was also the subject of a series of articles in the *Denver Post*. "In reality," says *Post* reporter Doug Oplinger, "disclosures of school violence vary wildly from one district to another. Some schools report every punch thrown on the playground. Others did not include assaults that police classified as felonies."[24] During his investigation, Oplinger learned that among schools that reported no violence or fights of any kind, one boy had suffered severe head wounds and a girl was hospitalized with bruised kidneys. Other incidents that were not reported included a sexual assault, a knifing, and attacks with a flagpole and baseball bat.

Teachers Under Attack

Violence against teachers is also a problem in many schools. The Bureau of Justice Statistics says that the greatest number of teacher-focused violent acts occur in city schools, rather than suburban, town, or rural schools. Also, public school teachers are at least 5 times more likely to be threatened than private school educators and 4 times more likely to be attacked. One city where violence is a serious problem in schools is Pontiac, Michigan. According to a study by Chartwell Education Group, the number of physical assaults in Pontiac schools increased from 15 in 2003–2004 to 184 in 2005–2006. In March 2008 science teacher Mark Taylor was brutally beaten by 3 students at Pontiac Northern High School, and the attack left him with a fractured skull, broken rib, and partially collapsed lung. "Teachers are in a war zone, and we should be getting combat pay," says Irma Collins, president of the Pontiac Education Association. "Teachers are scared going into their jobs every day, in both the middle schools and high schools."[25]

On April 1, 2008, some third graders from Waycross, Georgia, were arrested for plotting to attack their teacher. Police seized a steak knife with a broken handle, steel handcuffs, duct tape, and a crystal paperweight, among other items, and said the plot represented a serious threat. According to Waycross police chief Tony Tanner, the students intended to use the paperweight to knock the teacher unconscious; then they planned to bind her with the handcuffs and tape, and stab her with

> According to a December 2007 article in the *Baltimore Sun*, teachers and administrators throughout the country say they have been discouraged from reporting violent incidents in order to avoid the negative designation.

the knife. Each of the students involved was assigned a role, including taking part in the attack, covering the windows so no one could see in, and cleaning up afterward. "We did not hear anybody say they intended to kill her, but could they have accidentally killed her? Absolutely," says Tanner. "We feel like if they weren't interrupted, there would have been an attempt. Would they have been successful? We don't know."[26]

An Unfortunate Reality

Although violent acts such as shooting rampages are rare in schools, school violence can happen anywhere, at any time, to anyone. Small, rural village schools have been the site of violence, as have large inner city schools and sprawling college campuses. Students of all ages, ethnic backgrounds, and religions have been victims of school violence, and so have teachers and administrators. No matter who it touches, or the circumstances behind it, violence inevitably leaves fear and uncertainty in its wake.

Primary Source Quotes*

How Widespread Is School Violence?

"The decline in episodes of school-associated violence is promising and encouraging."

—Ileana Arias, quoted in Gail Hayes, "New Study Finds Decline in Single-Victim School-Associated Violent Deaths," Centers for Disease Control and Prevention, January 17, 2008. www.cdc.gov.

Arias is director of the Centers for Disease Control and Prevention's Injury Center.

"For the U.S. Department of Education to tell the American education community and public in general that school crime is declining is misleading."

—Neal McCluskey, "Violence in Public Schools: A Dirty Secret," The Heartland Institute, June 1, 2005. www.heartland.org.

McCluskey is a policy analyst at the Cato Institute's Center for Educational Freedom.

Bracketed quotes indicate conflicting positions.

* Editor's Note: While the definition of a primary source can be narrowly or broadly defined, for the purposes of Compact Research, a primary source consists of: 1) results of original research presented by an organization or researcher; 2) eyewitness accounts of events, personal experience, or work experience; 3) first-person editorials offering pundits' opinions; 4) government officials presenting political plans and/or policies; 5) representatives of organizations presenting testimony or policy.

Primary Source Quotes

66 **School is one of the safest places for children in the United States and . . . fewer than 1 percent of violent deaths of children occur at school. In fact, the most likely place for children to be murdered is in their own homes.** 99

—Scott Poland, "Keeping Schools Open After Violence," *District Administration*, December 2007.

Poland is chair of the National Emergency Assistance Team for the National Association of School Psychologists and a faculty member at Nova Southeastern University.

66 **Your kids are much more likely to be safer in school than they are at the mall. . . . We are, however, seeing some indications in the last two years that those trends are changing.** 99

—Alberto Gonzales, quoted in Gail Russell Chaddock, "How to Make US Schools Safer," *Christian Science Monitor*, October 12, 2006. www.csmonitor.com.

Gonzales is a former attorney general of the United States.

66 **We would like to think that institutions of learning and of rational thought would be spared such madness. Sadly, this is not the case in today's world.** 99

—Charles Steger, quoted in Kevin Bohn, "Company: Gunman, Virginia Tech Shooter Used Same Web Dealer," CNN.com, February 15, 2008. www.cnn.com.

Steger is president of Virginia Polytechnic Institute and State University.

66 **Even though the news has been filled with reports of school shootings lately, murders in schools are actually lower than in previous years. And the majority of children are safe at school.** 99

—Jodi Dworkin, "What If the Next Shooting Is at My School?" *Teen Talk*, University of Minnesota Extension Service. www.extension.umn.edu.

Dworkin is assistant professor in the Department of Family Social Science and the University of Minnesota Extension Service.

> ❝The vast majority of students are behaving themselves and are focused on learning. What makes the news are the ones who don't.❞

—Ed Pratt-Dannals, quoted in Tia Mitchell, "Moving Closer to Safer Schools," *Florida Times Union*, December 2, 2007.

Pratt-Dannals is superintendent of schools in Duval County, Florida.

> ❝When 8-year-olds are putting guns in their backpacks, perhaps people will take notice and demand solutions.❞

—Daniel Gross, quoted in Daryl Presgraves, "National Gun Violence Prevention Organization Demands Solutions After 8-Year-Old Boy Shoots 7-Year-Old Girl at Daycare," PAX, January 26, 2006. www.paxusa.org .

Gross is the founder of the antiviolence group PAX.

> ❝Students live in an ivory tower. The real world is a lot worse than these people realize. They are whining and crying, but there is a lot worse going on right now in our world than what happened at Virginia Tech. It wasn't even the first mass killing at a school.❞

—Nathan Jones, quoted in Lauren Boyer, "Students Defend Costume Choice," *Daily Collegian*, December 10, 2007. www.collegian.psu.edu.

Jones was a student at Penn State University who was widely criticized for appearing at a Halloween party in 2007 dressed in a blood-stained Virginia Tech shirt with fake bullet holes in his head.

> ❝We estimate that one-third of all colleges and universities in the U.S. either underreport or downplay crimes on campus.❞

—Alison Kiss, quoted in Stephanie Booth, "Why Your Campus Can Be a Danger Zone," *Cosmopolitan*, January 2008.

Kiss is program director of Security on Campus, a nonprofit campus crime prevention and victim assistance organization in King of Prussia, Pennsylvania.

66 School administrators should understand that most school weapons assaults bear no resemblance to the high profile multi-victim school shootings highlighted in the media. Most school weapons assaults are not preplanned events and are not fatal. 99

—Michael Dorn, "Preventing School Weapons Assaults," *Doors and Hardware*, March 2008.

Dorn is executive director of Safe Havens International, a nonprofit school safety center.

66 A lot of people my age think that bad things happen to everyone but them. I know now that stuff like this can happen. 99

—Emily Haas, quoted in Jill Smolowe, "Virginia Tech: The Hope and the Sorrow," *People Weekly*, September 3, 2007.

Haas is a student at Virginia Tech University who suffered minor head wounds during the school's April 2007 shooting.

How Widespread Is School Violence?

- According to the Bureau of Justice Statistics, **78 percent** of schools in the United States experienced one or more violent incidents of crime during the 2005–2006 school year, and **17 percent** experienced one or more serious violent incidents.

- The deadliest school shooting in U.S. history occurred on April 17, 2007, at Virginia Polytechnic Institute and State University in Blacksburg, Virginia, when **27 students** and **5 faculty members** were killed.

- The CDC reports that less than **1 percent** of all youth homicides occur at school.

- The Department of Justice says that children are **50 times** more likely to be murdered away from school than at school.

- During the 2006–2007 school year, there were **68 violent firearm-related deaths** at schools and colleges in the United States; 33 resulted from the April 2007 Virginia Tech shooting massacre.

- Roughly **13 percent** of public high school students in the United States reported that they had been involved in a fight at school during the 2006–2007 school year.

- About **8 percent** of public high school students in the United States said they had been threatened or injured with a weapon at school during the 2006–2007 school year.

Violent Deaths at School

Although the number of violent deaths* in U.S. elementary and secondary schools has fluctuated from 1992–2006, the trend was downward and the total during the 2005–2006 school year was 63 percent lower than it was during the 1992–1993 school year.

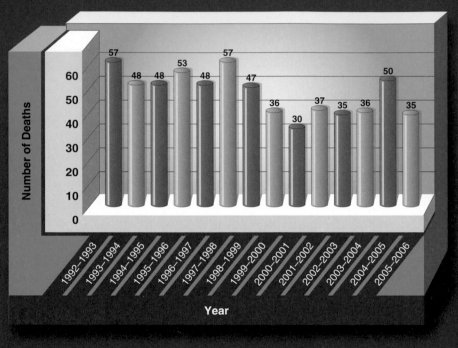

*School-associated violent deaths include homicides, suicides, legal intervention (involving a law enforcement officer), or unintentional fireman-related death in which the fatal injury occurred on the campus of a functioning elementary or secondary school in the United States, while the victim was on the way to or from regular sessions at school or while the victim was attending or traveling to or from an official school-sponsored event.

Source: U.S. Department of Justice and National Center for Education Statistics, "Indicators of School Crime and Safety," December 2007.

- National statistics suggest that about **20 percent** of students engage in some sort of violent or aggressive behavior in a typical school year.

- A 2007 report by AnComm showed that **stress, bullying, and depression** ranked number one, two, and three respectively, in a list of incidents reported by elementary, middle, and high school students.

- The Department of Justice reports that between 1993 and 2005 the percentage of students in grades 9 through 12 who reported **carrying a weapon** to school in the past month declined from **12 percent to 6 percent**.

Majority of Students Feel Very Safe at School

Research has shown that young people are safer in school than they are in the mall, on the street, in cars, or even in their own homes. According to a Harris poll conducted in November 2006, students agree. This chart shows how youths* aged 8 to 18 answered when asked the question:

"Overall, how safe do you feel when you are at school?"

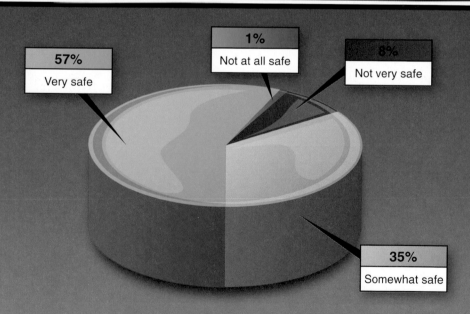

57% Very safe

1% Not at all safe

8% Not very safe

35% Somewhat safe

*Poll participants included 1,114 youth between the ages of 8 and 18 who attend school and are not home schooled.

Source: Harris Interactive, "Intruders in Our Public Schools: Two-Thirds of Youth and Three-Quarters of Parents Find It Likely That an Intruder Could Enter a School," December 12, 2006. www.harrisinteractive.com.

Crimes at School That Result in Arrests Increasing

According to an October 2007 report by the FBI, crime that occurs in America's schools and colleges is "one of the most troublesome societal problems in the nation today." From 2000 to 2004, arrests rose significantly for the most serious school-related offenses.

Crime	2000	2001	2002	2003	2004
Simple assault	6,436	9,136	10,120	11,550	14,220
Aggravated assault	1,009	1,228	1,291	1,427	1,531
Intimidation	830	1,631	1,327	1,434	1,776
Forcible fondling	231	300	357	341	446
Forcible rape	48	55	31	65	60
Kidnapping/Abduction	43	66	78	80	107
Forcible sodomy	19	20	23	20	22
Sexual assault with object	12	10	34	26	36
Statutory rape	9	13	11	16	30
Murder and nonnegligent manslaughter	1	7	7	7	5

Source: U.S. Department of Justice, FBI, Criminal Justice Information Services Division, "The CARD Report: Crime in Schools and Colleges," October 2007.

- A 2005 report by National School Safety and Security Services showed that **86 percent** of the school officers surveyed said that crimes at their schools were underreported, and **78 percent** said they had personally taken weapons from students in the past year.

- According to the CDC, most **school-associated violent deaths** occurred during transition times such as the start or end of the school day or during the lunch period, and school-associated homicides are most likely to occur at the start of each semester.

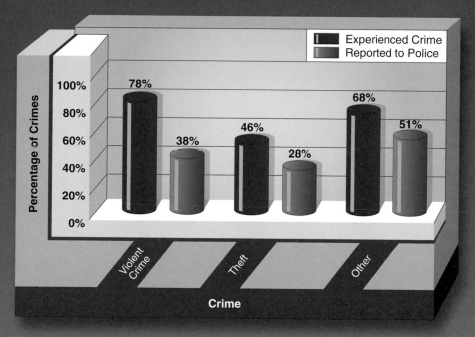

School Crimes Committed Versus Crimes Reported

By federal law, schools are required to report crime and violent incidents* to law enforcement—but according to a 2007 report by the U.S. Bureau of Justice Statistics and the National Center for Educational Statistics, discrepancies exist between crimes that occur and those that are actually reported. This graph illustrates such discrepancies during the 2005–2006 school year.

Experienced Crime
Reported to Police

Percentage of Crimes

100%
80%
60%
40%
20%
0%

78%
38%
46%
28%
68%
51%

Violent Crime
Theft
Other

Crime

*Violent incidents include rape or attempted rape, sexual battery other than rape, physical attack or fight with or without a weapon, threat of physical attack with or without a weapon, and robbery with or without a weapon. Other incidents include possession of a firearm or explosive device; possession of a knife or sharp object; distribution, possession, or use of illegal drugs or alcohol; and vandalism.

Source: U.S. Department of Justice and National Center for Education Statistics, "Indicators of School Crime and Safety," December 2007.

- According to the FBI's October 2007 "Crime in School and Colleges" report, of the 394,173 school crime offenders whose race was known, white offenders accounted for **71.1 percent** (280,178); black offenders, **27.4 percent** (107,878); and all other races combined, less than **2 percent** (6,117).

What Are the Causes of School Violence?

> **❝I honestly do not think it was on his mind to shoot all those people on the day he bought that gun. . . . Something had to set him off. . . . But whatever it was, he just snapped.❞**
>
> —John Markell, quoted in Elaine Shannon, "Where Cho Bought His Deadly Weapon."

> **❝Children who attack can be any age and from any ethnic group, race, or family situation. Contrary to assumptions that some of our youth 'just snap'—they don't. They plan.❞**
>
> —Debra Whitcomb, "Kids, Prosecutors, and Domestic Violence."

W henever a school shooting or other act of violence occurs, people desperately search for answers. They want to know how such a thing could have happened, what caused it, if it was prefaced by warning signs, and whether it could have been prevented. Although no simple answers exist, many experts have formed theories about the causes of school violence. Laurence Miller offers one of his own: "The cycle of violence typically begins when the student undergoes an event or series of events that he perceives as the 'last straw' in a cumulative series of humiliation. . . . The student isolates himself from the input of others and enters a mode of self-protection and self-justification in which a violent act may come to be perceived as 'the only way out.'"[27]

The Connection Between Bullying and School Violence

Because some of the worst acts of school violence are committed by students who have been bullied, a growing number of schools are starting to treat bullying as a serious offense. The seriousness of this problem gained widespread attention after the Columbine shooting massacre in April 1999. Afterward, students acknowledged that Eric Harris and Dylan Klebold had repeatedly been verbally and physically abused by kids who were part of the "in crowd," and that school officials were either oblivious to it or did nothing to stop it. Brooks Brown, who was friends with Harris and Klebold for years and was a classmate at Columbine, is outspoken in his belief that it is crucial for schools to identify and help kids who are troubled. "They actually share all the same red flags," he says. "The run-ins with the police, the violent writing, the threats on other students, the dark behavior. All of that screams. The real signs are that these kids feel hopeless—they are angry as hell."[28]

In the years since the Columbine tragedy, numerous violent acts in schools have been linked to troubled students who have been bullied. One occurred on September 29, 2006, when 15-year-old Eric Hainstock shot and killed John Klang, the principal of Weston School in Cazenovia, Wisconsin. Hainstock told investigators that he was upset because Klang had reprimanded him

> He said the kids in school called him names, stuck his head in the toilet, stuffed him in lockers, and threw him in the bushes.

for bringing tobacco to school. But at his trial, it was revealed that Hainstock had been the victim of constant bullying by classmates. He said the kids in school called him names, stuck his head in the toilet, stuffed him in lockers, and threw him in the bushes, and he just wanted the cruelty to stop. His friend testified that Hainstock had complained to Klang 20 or 30 times about the bullying but nothing was ever done.

Two months after the Wisconsin shooting, a young man from Germany also committed an act of violence at school—and he, too, had long been a victim of bullying. On November 20, 2006, 18-year-old Sebastian Bosse stormed into his former high school in Emsdetten, Germany, dressed in black and wearing a gas mask. He carried two sawed-off rifles and a pistol and had three bombs strapped to his body, a knife attached to his leg, and other explosives in his backpack. Upon entering the school he immediately began firing, and by the time he took his own life, 37 people had been wounded. Later, prosecutors found that Bosse had detailed his plans on a Web site that featured videoclips and pictures of him wearing

> **Many people attribute school violence, and youth violence in general, to the breakdown of families.**

military-style combat gear and holding a submachine gun. When a farewell message was discovered on an Internet forum, it became apparent that Bosse had planned the attack for weeks: "If you realize you'll never find happiness in your life and the reasons for this pile up day by day, the only option you have is to disappear from this life," he wrote. "The only thing I learned intensively at school was that I'm a loser. I hate you and the way you are! You've all got to die! . . . I'm gone."[29]

With the growing popularity of MySpace, FaceBook, and other teen-focused Web sites, as well as chat rooms and online discussion forums, bullying is becoming more high-tech. According to the CDC, young people use electronic media to embarrass their peers, as well as to harass and threaten them. The CDC reports:

> Increasing numbers of adolescents are becoming victims of this new form of violence. Although many different terms—such as *cyberbullying, Internet harassment,* and *Internet bullying*—have been used to describe this type of violence, *electronic aggression* is the term that most accurately captures all types of violence that occur electronically. Like traditional forms of youth violence, electronic aggression is associated with emotional distress and conduct problems at school.[30]

In one particular instance, online bullying led to tragedy. When Ryan Halligan was in middle school, a classmate pretended to befriend him online, and then later spread rumors via the Internet that he was gay. A popular female classmate engaged Ryan in instant messaging conversations pretending to like him. Then she embarrassed and humiliated him by sharing their private correspondence with other classmates and by telling him that she would never want anything to do with him because he was a loser. Ryan eventually became so despondent that he killed himself. His parents later said they did not blame their son's suicide solely on bullying, because he clearly had other problems. But they remain convinced that bullying and cyberbullying played a significant role in his deepening depression and his inability to cope with the pain in his life.

What Role Do Families Play?

Many people attribute school violence, and youth violence in general, to the breakdown of families. They say if more families communicated with each other and parents were more involved in their children's lives, violent behaviors could likely be avoided. After a deadly May 2007 shooting at a high school in Toronto, Canada, a survey of more than 1,000 people showed that one-third believed "absent, lax or poor parenting as the root cause of school violence. About one-quarter of those polled said they believe a 'lack of morals, conscience and respect' are to blame"[31] Dysfunctional family life has also been linked to bullying behavior in children. According to a study by scientists at York University and Queens University, which appeared in the March/April 2008 issue of the journal *Child Development*, children who bullied typically experienced a lot of conflict in relationships with their parents.

> **Gun control advocates argue that guns are far too easy for people to get, which means that many would-be killers have no problem purchasing them.**

An important component of family dynamics is that children who experience violence, abuse, or neglect are likely to become violent themselves. As Louise Last writes in *AllPsych Journal*:

School violence does not start in the school. Most behaviors are learned responses to circumstances and situations that are exhibited in our everyday life. Home life conditions are influences on all children. If a child grows up in a home where one of the parents is abused, whether verbally or physically, the child will take this as the norm. Studies have proven that a child living in an abusive home will himself become an abuser. Children who see violence view it as a solution to the problem. They see the stronger of the two components as the winner in the situation, and want to emulate the behavior.[32]

Parents who are oblivious to what their children are doing or have no idea that they are capable of violent acts are another factor in school violence. After the Columbine shooting, the parents of Klebold and Harris said they were not aware that the boys had been stockpiling guns and ammunition in their bedrooms, or that they had been building pipe bombs in the garage. Also, before the shooting happened, an employee of Green Mountain Guns called Harris's home; when the elder Harris answered, the employee said "Hey, your clips are in."[33] On a video made weeks prior to the shooting and discovered afterward, Eric Harris said if someone had checked into that message further, the massacre plans would have been ruined.

Too Many Guns?

Whenever there is a tragic shooting, whether in a school or elsewhere, the issue of guns is widely debated. Gun control advocates argue that guns are far too easy for people to get, which means that many would-be killers have no problem purchasing them. As Vincent Schiraldi, founder of the Center on Juvenile and Criminal Justice, explains: "It's nuts to think that kids are any crazier today than they ever were before; I think they're just better armed."[34]

John Markell, the firearms dealer whose employee sold a pistol to Virginia Tech gunman Seung-Hui Cho, said there was no reason to suspect that Cho intended to use the gun to commit an act of violence. Markell says that Cho was quiet and well mannered and did not seem at all suspicious. He presented three forms of identification and sailed through the background check with the Virginia State police computer system. Within minutes, he left the store with his rapid-firing Glock 9mm semiautomatic pistol. He purchased a second pistol from online firearms dealer Eric Thompson—and in a weird twist of fate, Northern Illinois University gunman Stephen Kazmierczak bought ammunition and a holster from another Web site operated by the same dealer. After learning about this, Thompson vowed to take a more active role in protecting the public, especially young people, from future attacks. "I've spent the past weekend feeling absolutely terrible that my company has been linked to both of these heinous crimes," he says. "I assume it is just an unfortunate coincidence, but I also believe I now have a special responsibility to do all I can to try and prevent further loss of life."[35]

John E. Rosenthal, who describes himself as a "gun owner and a staunch supporter of the Second Amendment," says that it is long past the time when national gun laws need to be strengthened. He explains:

> Sadly, gun laws have only been weakened since the massacres at Columbine High School and Virginia Tech. . . . Current federal law allows an unlimited number of easily concealable handguns and military-style weapons to be sold privately in 32 states without a criminal background check or an ID. Why do we take such a hands-off approach to these dangerous weapons? . . . You have to show ID to purchase alcohol or cigarettes. But if you want a Barrett .50-caliber sniper rifle (capable of penetrating steel and taking out an armored vehicle from more than a mile) you need only to show up at one of 5,000 legal gun shows and fork over the cash—no ID or background check required![36]

Can Violent Acts Be Prevented?

Although people may not necessarily agree about what causes school violence, most experts are convinced that many violent acts can be prevented. In many cases, students hear about threats ahead of time. If this sort of information were passed along to authorities, many tragedies could be prevented—but that, unfortunately, does not happen often enough. Either in fear of being called a "snitch" or the authorities failing to take the person's claims seriously, students often remain quiet about what they have been told. As psychologist Adele M. Brodkin explains, "Most individuals disturbed enough to kill do express hints of what they are planning. We all need to become aware of possible threats, and not dismiss them because they may be unthinkable to us."[37]

Students at Lincoln-Sudbury Regional High School in Sudbury, Massachusetts, had long suspected that 16-year-old John Odgren was capable of violence. Although the special education student had no official record of violent behavior, he often boasted of violence, telling classmates that he kept a gun at home and had once tried to kill someone. Odgren had reportedly chased a student while holding a shard of glass, threatened another with a screwdriver he had in his pocket, and told classmates that he knew how to commit the perfect murder. Fellow student Jason Pandolfi said he once observed Odgren using the school computer to search for information on making homemade bombs. Even with these warning signs, however, no one reported Odgren's behavior to school authorities—and on January 20, 2007, he acted on his threats. After cornering 15-year-old James Alenson in a school bathroom, Odgren took a carving knife out of his pocket and repeatedly stabbed the boy in the neck, rib cage, and abdomen. Alenson died from his wounds, and in a notebook that was recovered later, Odgren had written, "If it looks like murder it was . . . if it looks like an accident, it wasn't."[38]

> " Although people may not necessarily agree about what causes school violence, most experts are convinced that many violent acts can be prevented. "

No Simple Explanation

Whether it involves beatings, knife attacks, or shootings, school violence is a complicated, difficult issue—one for which there are no clear-cut solutions. The causes range from mental instability to dysfunctional family life, and the problem is exacerbated by bullying, the ready availability of weapons, and the reluctance of students to speak up when they suspect a classmate might be capable of violence. Psychologists, educators, and law enforcement officials are continuously seeking better ways of identifying the root causes of school violence. By gaining a greater understanding of the problem, expanding public awareness of it, and learning more about the psychology behind violent behavior, they hope eventually to find the key to preventing school violence before it happens.

Primary Source Quotes*

What Are the Causes
of School Violence?

> **66** He was an outstanding student, he was someone re-vered by the faculty and staff and students alike. So we had no problems and we've had no indications at all that this would be the type of person that would engage in such activity. **99**

—Donald Grady, quoted in ABC News.com, "NIU Rampage: No Motive, 5 Victims Dead," February 15, 2008.
http://abclocal.go.com.

Grady, the DeKalb, Illinois, police chief, in reference to Stephen Kazmierczak, a former Northern Illinois University student who shot and killed five NIU students on February 14, 2008.

> **66** The profile of the gun-toting student in a trench coat is just one of the myths about the rare but murderous attacks in the nation's schools. . . . In fact, there is no profile. **99**

—Bill Dedman, "10 Myths About School Shootings," MSNBC, October 10, 2007. www.msnbc.msn.com.

Dedman is a Pulitzer Prize–winning investigative journalist.

Bracketed quotes indicate conflicting positions.

* Editor's Note: While the definition of a primary source can be narrowly or broadly defined, for the purposes of Compact Research, a primary source consists of: 1) results of original research presented by an organization or researcher; 2) eyewitness accounts of events, personal experience, or work experience; 3) first-person editorials offering pundits' opinions; 4) government officials presenting political plans and/or policies; 5) representatives of organizations presenting testimony or policy.

Primary Source Quotes

66 Schools that allow bullying to continue are promoting violence. Studies show that acts of serious school violence often have their roots in bullying issues. **99**

—Hilda Clarice Quiroz et al., "Bullying in Schools," National School Safety Center. www.schoolsafety.us.

Quiroz is a program developer and training specialist at the National School Safety Center.

66 So if you aren't allowed to wear a hat, toot your horn, form a clique or pick on a freshman, all because everyone is worried that someone might snap, it's fair to ask: Are high schools preparing kids for the big ugly world outside those doors—or handicapping them once they get there? **99**

—Nancy Gibbs, "A Week in the Life of a High School," *Time*, October 25, 1999.

Gibbs is a journalist who writes for *Time* magazine.

66 Most attackers had previously used guns and had access to them, but access to weapons is not the most significant risk factor. **99**

—National Association of School Psychologists, "Threat Assessment: Predicting and Preventing School Violence." www.nasponline.org.

NASP supports school psychology programs and psychologists to enhance the learning and mental health of young people.

66 Let's get real about this: the problem is guns. If [a school shooter] had a knife, he wouldn't have been able to do the damage he did so quickly. **99**

—Jeffrey Claridge, quoted in Joan Raymond, "Troubled 'from Day One,'" *Newsweek*, October 22, 2007. www.newsweek.com.

Claridge is a trauma surgeon at MetroHealth Medical Center in Cleveland.

66 **They're youngsters who were feeling abused, being threatened in school, being bullied, and they felt helpless.** 99

—David Damore, quoted in Claire Metz, "Teens Charged in Alleged School Slaying Plot," MSNBC, April 1, 2008. www.msnbc.msn.com.

Damore is an attorney who is defending one of three Florida middle-schoolers accused in an alleged mass murder plot.

66 **While some school shooters were partially motivated by being bullied, to zero in on just the bullying misses the point. . . . Certainly bullying could be the thing that causes the blow up, but it could be any event that lights the fuse.** 99

—Ruth Wells, "The Surprising Truth About Bullying and Bullies," *Education Articles*, May 6, 2006. www.edarticle.com.

Wells is the director of Youth Change, an organization devoted to helping problem kids.

66 **You say that antidepressants are effective. So why did they not help Eric Harris before he shot me? . . . We should consider antidepressants to be accomplices to murder.** 99

—Mark Taylor, quoted in Christine Mangan, "Anti-Depressants to Blame for School Shootings?" Alpha Women, February 15, 2008. http://alphawomen.com.

Taylor, a Columbine shooting victim who nearly died from his wounds, testified before the FDA in 2004 that antidepressants were responsible for Eric Harris's rage.

66 **There is no scientific evidence to suggest that Zoloft contributes to violent behavior in either adults or children.** 99

—Officials from Pfizer, quoted in Elizabeth Cohen and Jim Polk, "Boy Told Police His Grandparents 'Deserved to Die,'" CNN Law Center, February 1, 2005. www.cnn.com.

Pfizer is one of the largest pharmaceutical companies in the world.

66 School shootings . . . are a symptom of a deep wound experienced by many students, a wound to the soul. School shootings are a cry of the soul. Look at me! Understand me! Love me! 99

—Michael Reist, "Dysfunctional Schools and Kids Who Kill," *Catholic New Times*, October 29, 2006.

Reist is an educator, speaker, and writer.

66 I would argue that discipline in our schools earlier is not working. And young men, in particular, are not internalizing the norms and values of our society. And periodically, you get acute manifestations of this, as in these rampage school shootings. 99

—Richard Arum, quoted in Lou Dobbs, "Death and Violence Are Not Rites of Passage," CNN.com, April 18, 2007.
www.cnn.com.

Arum is a professor of sociology and education at New York University.

What Are the Causes of School Violence?

- The CDC reports that an estimated **30 percent** of sixth to tenth graders in the United States either have been a bully, a target of bullying, or both.

- A 2007 report by the National Center for Education Statistics showed that in 2005 **24 percent** of students surveyed said that there were gangs at their school, up from **21 percent** in 2003.

- A 2005 survey of more than **22,500** police chiefs and sheriffs throughout the United States showed that nearly **95 percent** believed criminals were able to obtain most any type of firearm by illegal means.

- According to the National Institute on Media and the Family, by the time a child is 18 years old, he or she will have witnessed **200,000 acts of violence** on television, including **40,000 murders**.

- As of 2008, according to United States law, an unlimited number of concealable handguns and military-style weapons could legally be sold in **32 states** without a criminal background check or an ID.

- According to the CDC, among the students who committed a school-related homicide, **20 percent** were known to be victims of bullying.

School Violence Due to Gangs Is Increasing

Cities all over the United States struggle with gangs, and gangs contribute to many incidents of school violence. According to the U.S. Bureau of Justice Statistics, students report that gang presence in schools has risen since 2001, with the biggest increase in urban schools.

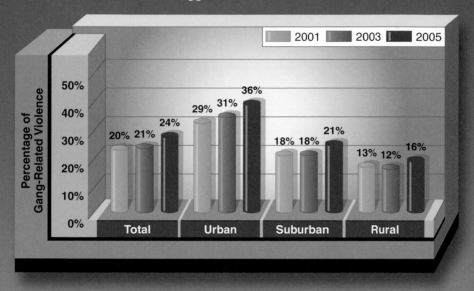

Source: U.S. Department of Justice and National Center for Education Statistics, "Indicators of School Crime and Safety," December 2007. http://nces.ed.gov.

- The CDC reports that **12 percent** of students who committed a school-related homicide were known to have expressed suicidal thoughts or engaged in suicidal behavior.

- The National Center for Educational Statistics reports that of students who said they had been bullied during the previous six months, **53 percent** said the bullying happened once or twice, **11 percent** said it happened once or twice a week, and **8 percent** said it happened almost daily.

- In one Philadelphia school district, special education students comprise **14 percent** of the student body but commit more than **40 percent** of all assaults on teachers and staff.

- Over **8 million** school-age kids are taking prescription antidepressants or other mood-altering drugs.

- One clinical trial of the antidepressant Prozac showed manic-type behavior in **6 percent** of the children studied.

Laws Against Bullying

As more attention has been given to solving the problem of school violence, more interest has been taken in bullying and the effect it may have on those who commit acts of violence. In 2002 the U.S. Secret Service released a report stating that bullying played a significant role in many school shootings and that efforts should be made to eliminate bullying behavior. As a way of solving the problem, more than half of the states have passed some type of antibullying legislation, and other states are considering it.

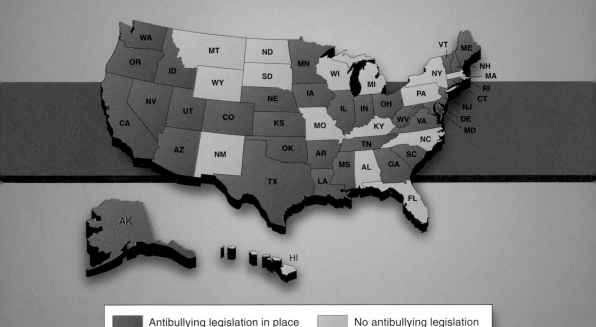

Antibullying legislation in place   No antibullying legislation

Sources: "School Bullying," National Conference of State Legislatures, March 2007. www.ncsl.org; Bully Police USA, "Does Your State Have an Anti-Bullying Law?" 2008. www.bullypolice.org.

Factors That Contribute to School Violence

Experts say school violence has many causes. There are four categories of potential contributors.

Individual Risk Factors

History of aggressive behavior or violence
Attention deficit, hyperactivity, or learning disorders
Problems with drugs or alcohol
Antisocial beliefs and attitudes
High emotional distress
Low IQ
History of treatment for emotional problems
Preoccupation with weapons or violence
Extreme mood swings

Family Risk Factors

Authoritarian childrearing attitudes
Harsh, lax, or inconsistent discipline
Low parental involvement, poor supervision
Low emotional attachment
Exposure to family violence
Parental substance abuse or criminality

VIOLENT BEHAVIOR

Peer/School Risk Factors

Involvement with gangs
Association with delinquent peers
Social rejection, harassment, bullying
Poor academic performance
Lack of involvement in hobbies and school activities
Low commitment to school and school failure

Community Risk Factors

Diminished economic opportunities
High poverty rate
High level of transience, family disruption
Low levels of community participation
Socially disorganized neighborhoods

Sources: CDC, "Youth Violence Fact Sheet," April 19, 2007. www.cdc.gov; Jodi Dworkin, "I'm Scared, What If the Next Shooting Is at My School?" University of Minnesota Extension Service, 2006. www.extension.umn.edu.

- In May 2008 a Missouri woman was indicted by a federal grand jury for using the **MySpace** site to cyberbully 13-year-old Megan Meier, who was so distraught that she **committed suicide** by hanging herself.

Prescription Medication Might Contribute to School Violence

It is now known that in numerous cases of violence, including school shootings, the perpetrators were taking prescription medications. No one knows if this contributed toward violent behavior, but the U.S. Food and Drug Administration does warn that violence and suicidal thoughts are possible side effects of antidepressants. Since 2001, prescriptions for chronic conditions have increased among adolescents.

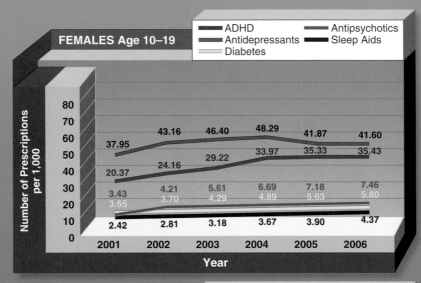

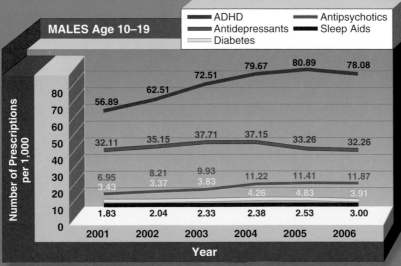

Source: Stacey Butterfield, "More Teens Are on Drugs–the Legend Kind," American College of Physicians Observer, November/December 2007. www.acponline.org.

What Is the Aftermath of School Violence?

> **"Even for survivors and their families, coping with the aftermath of violence is often a slow, imperfect process."**
>
> —Tamara Jones, "I Lived Through Virginia Tech."

> **"I want to issue a direct personal plea to all the major media: For the love of God and our children, stop broadcasting those images and those words. Choose to focus on life and the love and the light that our children brought into the world and not on the darkness and the madness and the death."**
>
> —Peter Reid, quoted in Richard E. Vatz and Lee S. Weinberg, "Any Lessons from Virginia Tech?"

When a heinous crime happens at a school, shock reverberates through the campus, the surrounding community, and even the entire nation. Families grieve for their lost loved ones, while survivors struggle with the horror of having watched their classmates and teachers be injured or die. Often those whose lives were spared are plagued with guilt, wondering if they could have done something to prevent the incident or to have saved people from being harmed. Even in faraway locations, those who have lived through violence in the past are often haunted by flashbacks. And for many who have been touched by a violent act, there is a sense that nothing will ever be quite the same. That is the perspective of Regina Rohde, a survivor of the Columbine High School shooting and who was also a student at Virginia Tech when the April 2007 shooting occurred. "People are living minute to minute, not being able to cope with anything in the future," she says. "Eventually it becomes hour to hour, week to week, where eventually, you can start planning . . . ahead in your life again. It takes a lot of time to pick those pieces back up again and continue on. Normalcy never comes back. It's a different definition of normal."[39]

Severe Emotional Trauma

On April 20, 1999, 15-year-old Erin Walton walked into Columbine High School, expecting it to be like any other normal school day—but it was far from normal, and the horror of what happened is permanently etched in her memory. Walton was in science class when she and other students heard banging and popping sounds, which they first assumed were just part of a senior prank. Then the terrifying reality of the situation struck them when they heard people screaming in the hallways, and teacher Dave Sanders stumbled into the classroom, bleeding profusely from wounds in his neck. Walton pulled off her sweatshirt and placed it on Sanders's neck in an attempt to stop the bleeding, while other students made a sign that they posted in the window to alert police and medical rescuers that they needed help. For more than three hours the students stayed in the classroom, trying to save their teacher's life while crouching in fear that the shooters would burst though the door at any second. Just before 3:00 P.M. help finally arrived, but it was too late for Sanders. Known as one of Columbine's

> "Walton pulled off her sweatshirt and placed it on Sanders's neck in an attempt to stop the bleeding, while other students made a sign that they posted in the window to alert police and medical rescuers that they needed help.

most popular teachers, he died from his injuries. Like many students who survived the tragedy, Walton remained haunted by it years later. "It's hard [for] me to think about going back to school," she says. "I can't be in a room with big windows."[40]

Columbine sophomore Marjorie Lindholm was in the science room with Walton that day, and she, too, was traumatized by what happened. For months afterward, she suffered from stomachaches, fevers, and horrible nightmares. Although she coped as best she could, a month into her senior year the former straight-A student dropped out of school because she could no longer handle being in a classroom. Later she struggled to get her life back, earning her GED and cowriting a book called *A Columbine Survivor's Story* with her mother. Today, because Lindholm is still afraid to be in a classroom, she is taking college classes online. Despite the years that have passed, she has not completely recovered, as she explains: "It took me years to be able to talk about it and now that I can talk about it, it's still like pouring salt in old wounds. It's very hard, because part of my day-to-day life is school and school is my one phobia now. It's the one place I'm really scared to be."[41]

> " Post-traumatic stress disorder can set in long after a violent event happens, crippling its victims with fear, flashbacks, and recurring nightmares. "

The lingering fear and uncertainty expressed by Walton and Lindholm is common among survivors of school violence. Although people may react differently to such crises and work through their pain and grief in their own way, the emotional scars often last for years and sometimes never completely disappear. Post-traumatic stress disorder can set in long after a violent event happens, crippling its victims with fear, flashbacks, and recurring nightmares. Frank DeAngelis, the principal of Columbine High School during the 1999 shootings, says he has seen people who seem to be coping well for five years or more have a breakdown when they hear about a current act of school violence. He describes how he felt when learning about what happened at Virginia Tech:

Sick to my stomach, just gut wrenching, gut wrenching. Even though it was happening at Virginia Tech, I was having flashbacks to Columbine High School, having flashbacks to our students running out of the building with their hands on top of their head being escorted by the SWAT team. When I saw students falling from the windows, in my mind, I saw Patrick Ireland [shooting victim known as the "boy in the window"] on that day, and so it was very difficult for me.[42]

"It's a Question of Accountability"

Once the initial shock of a violent act wears off, families of victims are often left feeling bitter and angry. They begin questioning whether something could have been done to stop it, and they wonder whether school officials and law enforcement handled the crisis properly. This was the case in April 2007, after the Virginia Tech shooting. At 7:15 A.M., when the first two people were shot inside West Ambler Johnston Hall, campus police responded within minutes. Officers secured the building and asked everyone inside to remain in their rooms for safety reasons. They questioned students and reached the conclusion that the shooting was an isolated incident, likely sparked by a domestic dispute. Classes went on as scheduled and more than two hours passed before Virginia Tech faculty and students received an e-mail about the shooting at the dormitory—and by that time, Seung-Hui Cho was continuing his rampage inside Norris Hall. Emergency e-mails went out telling people to stay inside buildings and keep away from windows, and an e-mail sent at 10:16 A.M. announced that classes were canceled. But in the end, 28 students and 5 faculty members were dead, and more than 24 others had been wounded. Parents of the victims were outraged over the 2-hour time lag between Cho's shootings, and they threatened to sue the university. If the school had locked down the campus immediately and communicated with students sooner, they said, the murders in Norris Hall might have been avoided. According to crime prevention expert Vincent Bove, a courtroom showdown is necessary to reveal what went wrong that day at Virginia Tech and expose who is to blame. "It's not a matter of money," he says, "it's a question of accountability. What needs to be brought to light is the lack of leadership, and that is more important than any amount of money. Virginia Tech failed the families who entrusted their children to them."[43]

Victims' families were also angry after Stephen Kazmierczak committed the shootings at Northern Illinois University. Although Kazmierczak was well liked by teachers and fellow students, an investigation after the killings showed that he had a history of mental problems. When he was a teenager his parents confined him to a Chi-

> Once the initial shock of a violent act wears off, families of victims are often left feeling bitter and angry.

cago mental institution, where he spent months undergoing intensive psychotherapy, and he had been on a variety of antidepressants and other medicines since that time. Yet in spite of Kazmierczak's disturbed past, he was able to buy four guns over a six-month period from a firearms store in Champaign, Illinois. Connie Catellani, a parent of an NIU student, explained how stunned she was at learning this: "Why was this tormented young man able to carry out this massacre? How could he legally obtain a weapon, designed to kill so many people in such a short time?"[44]

Healing Through Forgiveness

In October 2006 Charles Carl Roberts, a milk truck driver, walked into an Amish school in Nickel Mines, Pennsylvania, told the boys to leave, and then shot 10 young girls execution-style before killing himself. Five of the girls died and the others were seriously wounded, with one left paralyzed, unable to talk and having to be fed through a tube. Yet even though the victims' families were suffering from grief, they reached out to the killer's family, assuring them that they forgave the man. They also donated money to help set up a special fund so his children could go to college. Marie Roberts, wife of the gunman, issued a statement expressing her gratefulness for how the Amish people reached out to her. "Your love for our family has helped to provide the healing we so desperately need," she wrote. "Gifts you've given have touched our hearts in a way no words can describe. . . . Your compassion has reached beyond our family, beyond our community, and is changing our world, and for this we sincerely thank you."[45]

Forgiveness has also helped other school violence victims heal. Garrett

Evans, who was shot in the leg during the Virginia Tech shooting, says he bears no ill will toward Cho. In fact, he says that he feels sorry for the gunman and wishes he could have known him before so he could have reached out to him. "The key to healing, and the first step, the most important step, is to forgive," Evans says. "I forgive that shooter. I'm alive. I'm healing. I'm just so blessed. Words cannot describe how blessed I am."[46]

Copycat Crimes

One of the most disturbing repercussions after school violence occurs is that some people view the criminals as heroes. This is most often true with those who are emotionally unstable, feel victimized, and desperately long for attention. School violence experts suspected that a copycat crime had taken place after Roberts shot the girls in the Amish schoolhouse. The tragic incident was eerily similar to a shooting that had occurred just five days earlier at Platte Canyon High School in Bailey, Colorado. In both cases, suicidal gunmen released the boys from the room, lined up the girls against a blackboard, and shot them before killing themselves.

Copycatting was also suspected in the Virginia Tech shooting. Two days after it occurred, NBC News received a package that had been mailed by Cho, apparently between the first and second shooting sprees. Inside was a DVD that showed him wearing battle gear, holding guns, and talking angrily to the camera, along with a written manifesto in which he referred to Eric Harris and Dylan Klebold as martyrs. This, along with the many similarities between the two crimes, led school violence experts to conclude that Cho was inspired by the Columbine gunmen to commit his own act of violence. Cho's actions, in turn, inspired another alleged would-be killer. On March 25, 2008, 20-year-old Calin Chi Wong posted a message on an Internet forum in which he threatened to commit a school massacre like the one at Virginia

> " Two days later, police searched Wong's home and found 13 firearms, including 4 AK-47 assault rifles, and thousands of rounds of ammunition, some of which were capable of piercing armor. "

Tech. Using the screen name "thehumanabc," Wong wrote: "I'm soon to the point to re-enact the whole event. This may not seem like a threat to you, but I'm sure others don't want to see it occur again. It should be a wake up call for all haters out there."[47] Two days later police searched Wong's home and found 13 firearms, including four AK-47 assault rifles, and thousands of rounds of ammunition, some of which were capable of piercing armor. Although Wong told police that he never actually intended to go on a killing spree, he was arrested and charged with using the Internet to make threats to kill or do bodily injury.

The media are often criticized for the notoriety that perpetrators get after committing violent crimes. Their stories, accompanied by photos and often filled with gruesome details, are splashed across Web sites and blogs, as well as appearing on television news and front-page newspaper articles. This, many believe, creates the potential for copycat crimes to be committed by people who are envious of the criminals' fame. James Allan Fox, who is a professor of criminal justice in Boston, says that many school shooters are people who tend to identify with anyone who gets revenge by killing. He explains: "They see others who go on rampages in other schools as heroes. They're heroes because they got even with all the students and teachers and not only that, they're famous for it."[48]

"NIU Will Never Be the Same"

In the aftermath of school violence, people are often left feeling shocked, sad, fearful, and sometimes angry. They handle their grief in different ways; some are quick to forgive, while others hold on to their anger and lash out at others they feel are partly to blame. They may recover within months or suffer from emotional trauma and flashbacks for years. The one thing they all share in common is that even though they eventually heal, they will never forget what happened to them, or those whose lives were lost. As editors from Northern Illinois University's *Northern Star* explain: "It will be difficult and even unbearable for many, but we will do it and we will be stronger as a family for it. To the families and friends of those who have lost loved ones, NIU shares this pain as a family. NIU will never be the same, but we will NEVER forget those family members we must now live without. They will live on forever in our memories and in our hearts."[49]

Primary Source Quotes*

What Is the Aftermath of School Violence?

Primary Source Quotes

66 I know it doesn't seem like it will get better, but I promise it does. The pain fades. You don't forget about it, but the pain does fade, and it does get better, and there are little glimmers of hope that makes life worth living. It will get better. 99

—Emily Jacobson, quoted in Tom Bearden, "Survivors of Virginia Tech Shootings Face Long Road to Normalcy," *PBS, Online NewsHour*, April 25, 2007. www.pbs.org.

Jacobson was a student at Columbine High School during the April 1999 shootings.

66 There's not a day that goes by without us wishing that she was here and just remembering all the crazy things that we did and said together. It's been a year and I still sit there at 3:30 and wait for her to get off the bus. ... Even though it's been a year, I'm just devastated by it, by her being gone. 99

—Theresa Spike, quoted in Amy Forliti, "Victims Honored One Year After School Shooting," *Indian Country Today*, March 27, 2006. www.indiancountry.com.

Spike's daughter, Alicia White, was killed during the March 2005 shooting at the high school on the Red Lake Band of Chippewa's reservation in Minnesota.

* Editor's Note: While the definition of a primary source can be narrowly or broadly defined, for the purposes of Compact Research, a primary source consists of: 1) results of original research presented by an organization or researcher; 2) eyewitness accounts of events, personal experience, or work experience; 3) first-person editorials offering pundits' opinions; 4) government officials presenting political plans and/or policies; 5) representatives of organizations presenting testimony or policy.

❝I'm not scared to be back at all. We just have to move forward.❞

—Lindsey Bryant, quoted in Jill Smolowe, "Virginia Tech: The Hope and the Sorrow," *People Weekly*, September 3, 2007.

Bryant is a student at Virginia Tech University who was not injured in the April 2007 shooting at the school.

❝Some carry physical wounds: A missing eye, a disfigured hand. Many more have hidden scars: They cannot sleep, or bear the darkness. They cannot be alone.❞

—Terry Collins, "A Long Year at Red Lake: Still Haunted, but Healing," *Minneapolis Star Tribune*, May 8, 2006. www.startribune.com.

Collins, a journalist who writes for the *Minneapolis Star Tribune*, referring to the one-year anniversary of the shooting at the high school on the Red Lake Band of Chippewa's reservation in Minnesota.

❝Some people have made fun of me because I forgive the killers. I cannot hold them responsible because they were sick in the head.❞

—Mark Taylor Jr., quoted in Andrew Johnson, "Impact of School Shootings Called Worse than That of War," *Pittsburgh Tribune-Review*, October 5, 2006.

Taylor, a victim of the Columbine High School shootings who nearly died from his injuries, referring to the shooters Eric Harris and Dylan Klebold.

❝Incorporating this event into our lives, weaving it into who we are while not letting it define who we are, will continue for a very, very long time.❞

—Lynn Cook, quoted in Tamara Jones, "I Lived Through Virginia Tech," *Good Housekeeping*, December 2007.

Cook is the mother of Ally Cook, who recovered from serious gunshot wounds suffered during the Virginia Tech shooting in April 2007.

❝It's a tough way to become a strong community. But I'm very comfortable that in a few months, everyone here will look at each other and say we are a stronger community.❞

—Jonathan C. Perry, quoted in Ashley M. Heher, "Shooting Aftermath: NIU Moves Forward," WTOP News, February 23, 2008. www.wtop.com.

Perry is a clinical psychologist who led grief training sessions after the February 2008 shooting at Northern Illinois University.

❝I don't believe in happy endings. But maybe in the future, I will look to the past and say, 'That happened to me and I'm cool now.'❞

—Deion Mendez, quoted in Susan Snyder and Martha Woodall, "When Fear Is Part of School," *Philadelphia Inquirer*, June 11, 2006.

Mendez, a teenager from Philadelphia, was the victim of a vicious beating attack by fellow students as he was leaving school in January 2006.

❝One of the things that help children after a tragedy is routine. Having school canceled is a significant departure from the normal routine.❞

—Scott Poland, "Keeping Schools Open After Violence," *District Administration*, December 2007.

Poland is chair of the National Emergency Assistance Team for the National Association of School Psychologists and a faculty member at Nova Southeastern University.

❝'Why did you let us die?' he said [his bloody classmates] yelled. 'Why did you let him do that to us?' He showed no tears. But you could tell that it was eating him up inside.❞

—Cindy Lussier, quoted in Terry Collins, "A Long Year at Red Lake: Still Haunted, but Healing," *Minneapolis Star Tribune*, May 8, 2006. www.startribune.com.

Lussier, whose son's life was spared in the 2005 shooting at Red Lake High School, referring to the violent nightmares he suffered afterward.

❝It's natural for children to worry. But talking with children about these tragedies, and what they watch or hear about them, can help put frightening information into a more balanced context.❞

—Centers for Disease Control and Prevention, "Tips for Coping with Stress." www.cdc.gov.

The CDC, which is part of the U.S. Department of Health and Human Services, is America's leading public health organization.

❝I've never heard of a kid going to fourth grade with a gun. Usually it's in middle school or something that I hear that.❞

—Hector Seche, quoted in Tina Kelley, "Fourth Grader Is Suspended for Taking a Loaded Handgun to School in New Jersey," *New York Times*, November 29, 2007.

Seche was a fourth grader at Clinton Elementary School in Plainfield, New Jersey, when a fellow student was caught with a loaded semiautomatic handgun in his school locker.

What Is the Aftermath
of School Violence?

- In a spring 2006 survey by the Harvard School of Public Health, more than **25 percent** of high school students in Boston said they would not report a crime for fear of reprisal or being labeled a snitch.

- According to PAX, a 2007 survey showed that over **50 percent** of students would definitely or probably report a threat even if people would think they were a snitch.

- A survey by the National Association of Independent Schools showed that adults surveyed named **"safe"** as the second most important adjective to describe private schools.

- According to the Department of Justice, fewer students are avoiding places in school because of fear for their safety; between 1995 and 2005, the percentage of students who reported avoiding one or more places in school declined from **9 percent** to **4 percent**.

- After 18 Chicago public school students were killed by gunfire in a six-month period, the city's police became the first in the country with live access to the **4,500 security cameras** mounted inside and outside the city's schools.

- According to the U.S. surgeon general, most **youths involved in violent behavior** will never be arrested for a violent crime.

Post-Traumatic Stress Disorder

In an article published in April 2007, Dr. Laurence Miller writes, "The crisis is not over when the police and TV crews leave. Students or faculty may have been killed, others wounded, some held hostage, and many psychologically traumatized." Although everyone reacts to grief differently, emotional trauma is common among those who have lived through school violence, and some young people suffer from a serious form of stress known as post-traumatic stress disorder (PTSD). This chart shows the "symptom clusters" that are typically used in the diagnosis of PTSD in young people.

Symptom	Indicators
Recurring recollections of trauma	Intrusive thoughts, disturbing dreams, flashbacks, dissociative behavior (daydreaming, disorientation, focus on inner fantasy worlds), intense emotional and physiological distress when reexposed to stimuli associated with traumatic event.
Avoidance of trauma-associated stimuli ("numbing")	Sense of detachment, restricted range of emotions, dysphoria (anxiety, restlessness, sadness), loss of certain developmental skills, sense of foreboding about the future.
Persistent physiological hyper-arousal	Difficulties with sleeping, hypervigilance (increased arousal and attention to cues in external environment that may potentially be associated with threat, distraction, attention problems), trouble with concentration, increased startle response, impulsive behaviors, irritability, profound anger, increased physiological reactivity.

Sources: Laurence Miller, "School Violence: The Psychology of Youthful Mass Murder and What to Do About It," PoliceOne.com News, April 20, 2007. www.policeone.com; Bruce D. Perry, "Stress, Trauma, and Post-Traumatic Stress Disorders in Children: An Introduction," The Child Trauma Academy, 2002. www.childtrauma.org.

- Since the **Columbine shootings** in 1999, hundreds of schools throughout the United States have heightened security measures and put violence-prevention programs in place.

- An estimated **5 million** children are exposed to a traumatic event in the United States every year, amounting to **1.8 million** new cases of post-traumatic stress disorder.

School Shooting Deaths: 2006–2007

School shootings may be rare, but when they happen, the aftermath leaves people afraid, insecure, angry, and emotionally traumatized. This map shows the school shootings that occurred in the United States during 2006 and 2007, resulting in one or more deaths.

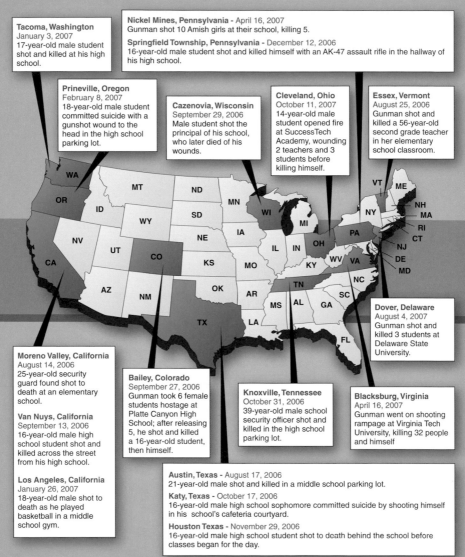

Tacoma, Washington
January 3, 2007
17-year-old male student shot and killed at his high school.

Nickel Mines, Pennsylvania - April 16, 2007
Gunman shot 10 Amish girls at their school, killing 5.

Springfield Township, Pennsylvania - December 12, 2006
16-year-old male student shot and killed himself with an AK-47 assault rifle in the hallway of his high school.

Prineville, Oregon
February 8, 2007
18-year-old male student committed suicide with a gunshot wound to the head in the high school parking lot.

Cazenovia, Wisconsin
September 29, 2006
Male student shot the principal of his school, who later died of his wounds.

Cleveland, Ohio
October 11, 2007
14-year-old male student opened fire at SuccessTech Academy, wounding 2 teachers and 3 students before killing himself.

Essex, Vermont
August 25, 2006
Gunman shot and killed a 56-year-old second grade teacher in her elementary school classroom.

Dover, Delaware
August 4, 2007
Gunman shot and killed 3 students at Delaware State University.

Moreno Valley, California
August 14, 2006
25-year-old security guard found shot to death at an elementary school.

Van Nuys, California
September 13, 2006
16-year-old male high school student shot and killed across the street from his high school.

Los Angeles, California
January 26, 2007
18-year-old male shot to death as he played basketball in a middle school gym.

Bailey, Colorado
September 27, 2006
Gunman took 6 female students hostage at Platte Canyon High School; after releasing 5, he shot and killed a 16-year-old student, then himself.

Knoxville, Tennessee
October 31, 2006
39-year-old male school security officer shot and killed in the high school parking lot.

Blacksburg, Virginia
April 16, 2007
Gunman went on shooting rampage at Virginia Tech University, killing 32 people and himself

Austin, Texas - August 17, 2006
21-year-old male shot and killed in a middle school parking lot.

Katy, Texas - October 17, 2006
16-year-old male high school sophomore committed suicide by shooting himself in his school's cafeteria courtyard.

Houston Texas - November 29, 2006
16-year-old male high school student shot to death behind the school before classes began for the day.

Source: National School Safety and Security Services, "School Deaths and School Shootings: 2006–2007." www.schoolsecurity.org.

Tighter Security Measures

In the aftermath of school shootings and other acts of violence in schools throughout the United States, administrators, security experts, and law enforcement have worked together to implement tighter security measures. This graph shows how the percentage of public schools with security and safety measures in place has risen since the 1999–2000 school year.

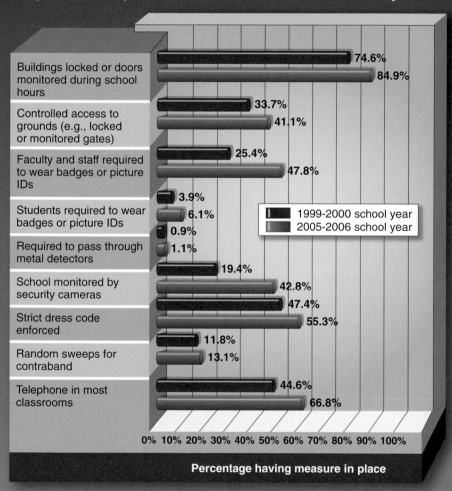

Measure	1999-2000 school year	2005-2006 school year
Buildings locked or doors monitored during school hours	74.6%	84.9%
Controlled access to grounds (e.g., locked or monitored gates)	33.7%	41.1%
Faculty and staff required to wear badges or picture IDs	25.4%	47.8%
Students required to wear badges or picture IDs	3.9%	6.1%
Required to pass through metal detectors	0.9%	1.1%
School monitored by security cameras	19.4%	42.8%
Strict dress code enforced	47.4%	55.3%
Random sweeps for contraband	11.8%	13.1%
Telephone in most classrooms	44.6%	66.8%

Percentage having measure in place

Source: "Indicators of School Crime and Safety," U.S. Department of Justice and National Center for Education Statistics, December 2007. http://nces.ed.gov.

- In a March 2007 survey by C.S. Mott Children's Hospital, adult participants were asked to rate 17 different health concerns for children, and **school violence was number 8**.

Can School Violence Be Stopped?

> 66 **There is no one program, no silver bullet, so that you can get one program up and say, here it is, if you put this program in your school, you are going to resolve school violence.** 99
>
> —William Modzeleski, quoted in Lisa Snell, "School Violence and No Child Left Behind: Best Practices to Keep Kids Safe."

> 66 **Because many schools have adopted safety procedures, school violence can often be prevented.** 99
>
> —Michael Tiede, quoted in Mayo Clinic, "School Violence: An Interview with a Mayo Clinic Specialist."

Keeping students safe in and around school is a major priority for educators, administrators, and law enforcement personnel. To stop school violence is a daunting task, however, because it is unpredictable and in many cases happens without warning. Safety expert Michael Dorn says that the first step toward prevention is to overcome the "it could never happen here" mindset. According to Dorn, even though shootings are extremely rare at schools, people need to be aware that "risk for this type of crime is present."[50] Although the media are often criticized for sensationalizing school violence, especially shootings, the positive side is that the publicity has increased awareness that violent acts can strike anywhere, at any time. This has spurred many school officials to put violence-prevention programs in place.

In the past, threatening statements made by students were often disregarded and not taken seriously, but that is changing rapidly. Security consultants and violence experts urge schools to view every single threat as potential for a real-life violent act to occur. Susan Gaertner, county attorney in Ramsey County, Minnesota, explains: "Maybe 20 years ago, we would write things like this off as boys will be boys or girls will be girls. We don't do that anymore. Kids need to understand that this kind of behavior will be taken seriously by the system, and there are serious consequences for threatening violence, particularly in a school setting."[51] In February 2008 a written threat led to an emergency lockdown of classrooms and buildings on the campus of St. Peter's College in Jersey City, New Jersey. School officials discovered a handwritten note taped to a hallway wall that referenced the Virginia Tech massacre, and they considered it a very realistic threat. "It sent chills down my spine," says St. Peter's president Eugene J. Cornacchia. "It was clearly written, and it was direct and to the point in what they were claiming was going to happen."[52] Within minutes of finding the note, officials used the school's new text-messaging alert system to notify students and staff about the lockdown, and then notified the Jersey City Police. Officers searched the campus, and once they had determined it was safe, the lockdown was lifted and police began investigating who might have issued the threat.

In April 2008 a 15-year-old student from Kempsville High School in Virginia Beach, Virginia, posted a threat on the MySpace site about taking a gun to school. A parent saw the threat about 3 hours after it was posted and reported it to police. Officers worked through the night to determine who the poster was, and by 2:00 A.M. they had identified him. He was arrested at his home, taken to a juvenile detention facility, and charged with threatening to kill or injure people on school property.

Breaking the Code of Silence

Security experts say that a major factor in stopping school violence is convincing students to speak up when they hear of a threat, witness acts of bullying, or observe anything that they consider suspicious. According to Daniel Gross, in as many as four out of five school shootings, the attackers have told other students about their plans beforehand, whether they intended to commit suicide or harm others. PAX, the organization founded by Gross, works to educate students about the importance of taking threats seriously and reporting them to school officials or law enforcement. Josh Stevens is aware of how important that is—but his awareness came too late. In 2001 when Stevens was 15 years old, his friend Charles Andrew "Andy" Williams told him that he planned to attack the school. Assuming that Williams was not serious, Stevens did nothing about it. The next day Williams made good on his threat: He took a gun to school and opened fire, killing 2 students and wounding 13 others. Today Josh says that not reporting his friend's threat was a mistake he will regret for the rest of his life. He explains: "He said he was going to pull a Columbine. I thought he was joking. He came to school and shot 15 students; 2 of them died. If I would have said something, none of this would have happened."[53]

> Security consultants and violence experts urge schools to view every single threat as potential for a real-life violent act to occur.

Students are often reluctant to report threats or crimes because they fear being labeled a snitch, and security experts are well aware of that. One program established by PAX, known as the Speak Up campaign, is designed to give people the opportunity to anonymously report weapon-related threats toll-free, 24 hours a day, 7 days a week. As of January 2008 Speak Up had received more than 20,000 calls, and according to Gross, these calls have resulted in hundreds of weapons being confiscated and numerous threats being averted. Students from the Olivet Boys and Girls Club in Reading and Berks County, Pennsylvania, are so serious about the Speak Up campaign that they are donating their time to produce 30-second video public service announcements for schools. Teen services director Judd Meinhart explains why the students are so enthusiastic about the project: "Speak Up is an excellent tool to combat the 'stop snitching' stigma perpetrated by today's pop culture. Educating teens and promoting the Speak Up hotline empowers youth to prevent tragedies like the ones that have occurred at schools and college campuses across the country."[54]

Another group that helps students report threats anonymously is known as AnComm, whose Talk About It program uses a Web-based portal to help young people report threats to trained administrators and counselors. Students use an ID number and password to sign in, and they are told up front that AnComm will only reveal their names to school officials if they appear to pose a serious threat to themselves or others. To date, 150,000 students in 18 states have access to the Talk About It service, and during the 2006–2007 school year, they reported nearly 6,000 incidents. One school district that uses Talk About It is the Manor Independent School District (ISD) in Manor, Texas. Superintendent Mark Diaz explains why the program is so effective:

Today Josh says that not reporting his friend's threat was a mistake he will regret for the rest of his life.

> We have prevented three suicides in Waco ISD. How can you value that? You don't know the value of this program because you don't see the number of suicides that I have experienced. All it takes is one, and then you'll join the program, but why wait?
>
> By this tool we have given them (students) the freedom to care enough and express their caring for their fellow students.
>
> It reinforces what we value the most in our lives. We want to create a school that is warm and inviting and threat free.[55]

Being Prepared for School Violence

Even though school administrators are aware that school shootings are rare, many are putting programs in place to prepare educators and students for acts of violence. Growing numbers of schools are putting together emergency task forces and holding drills. The state of Rhode Island, for instance, mandates that schools hold two evacuation drills and two lockdown drills per year. New York schools must conduct emergency drills at least once a year, and Michigan requires two annual lockdown drills. Some schools have put together drills that are highly realistic, with student and teacher actors pretending to be shooters and others playing the role of victims.

In February 2008 an elementary school in Round Valley, Arizona, was the site of this sort of realistic drill. School officials used makeup on third to fifth graders to simulate bullet wounds and other injuries and covered the students with fake blood. Actors playing "bad guys" wore face masks, took children and teachers as their "hostages," and got into shootouts with police using cap guns. As the drill was going on, teachers and administrators practiced a lockdown. When it was over, school officials said it had been a worthwhile experience and had benefited everyone by teaching them to be prepared for a real-life emergency.

A realistic drill was held in March 2008 at Elizabeth City State University in Indiana—but even though officials had sent out e-mails and text messages about the upcoming drill, many at the school did not get the messages and believed it was real. Just after 1:30 P.M. a campus police officer, playing the role of a gunman, walked into a classroom and told assistant professor Jingbin Wang that he wanted to talk to him. Then he pointed a fake gun at Wang, instructed him to close the door, and ordered him to line the students up along the wall. At one point the gunman threatened to kill the student with the lowest grade point average. Wang says that he had no idea it was a drill, and feeling the gun on his back he was fully prepared to die. In a nearby classroom, frightened students blocked the door with a table and chairs, and some were prepared to jump out of the window to escape to safety. After about 10 minutes, campus police rushed into the room and took the gunman away.

> Some were furious in the wake of the mock attack, saying that students could have been seriously injured trying to escape and the undercover officer himself could have been harmed or even killed.

When school officials learned that many had taken the drill seriously, they issued an apology and offered counseling to faculty and students who wanted it. Yet some were furious in the wake of the mock attack, saying that students could have been seriously injured trying to escape and the undercover officer himself could have been harmed or even killed. Later, student editors at the *Indiana Daily Student* released an editorial saying that the episode was cruel, and they issued a plea to university administrators: "We know you love us," they wrote. "We know you want us to be safe and well-prepared for emergencies on campus. But you don't have to stage armed intrusions into our classrooms to prove your dedication to campus safety."[56]

Could More Guns Reduce Gun Violence?

The issue of allowing guns on college campuses is highly controversial, with strong arguments on both sides. Many states have laws in place that make it illegal for anyone to carry a firearm at schools or universities, but some are pushing for legislation to change that. John F. McManus, president of the John Birch Society, supports allowing students and educators to be armed at colleges and universities as a way of deterring criminals from engaging in violent acts. He explains:

> If there's a lesson to be learned from this [school shooting] tragedy, and from similar tragedies, it is that no noncriminal should ever be denied the right to defend himself. The situation that developed at Virginia Tech could have been minimized by someone taking action against Cho. Of course, no one should be forced to carry a gun. But no one should be barred from having one either.[57]

> **Many states have laws in place that make it illegal for anyone to carry a firearm at schools or universities, but some are pushing for legislation to change that.**

Those who disagree with McManus argue that more guns on campus would naturally result in more violence and even more tragedies would occur. One with that perspective is Dewey Cornell, who believes it is a fallacy to assume that allowing students and teachers to be armed will result in safer campuses. He says:

> It is always tempting to imagine heroic scenarios where

someone with a gun comes to the rescue. We see it on [television] every night, but it is not realistic. More things can go wrong than go right. When we look at other nations we see that they have a much, much lower rate of gun violence than we do, yet this is not because their citizens are armed and ready to shoot the shooters. We need a more realistic understanding of the problem and not one that has been produced by all our years of watching television violence.[58]

Hope for the Future

Whether it involves beating, bullying, assault, shooting, or other weapons offenses, school violence is a serious problem. Although studies have shown that young people are safer in schools than they are on the streets, at the mall, or even in their own homes, that does not negate the fact that school violence is always a possibility. Educators, administrators, security experts, and law enforcement officials are working together to implement measures that keep students safe, educate them about school violence, and help prepare them for violent acts that could potentially occur. Will this sort of approach be able to stop school violence? No one knows the answer to that. But many agree that the reality of school violence must be faced because it can strike anywhere, at any time. Chris Lehmann, principal of a Philadelphia school, expresses how he feels whenever he hears about a violent tragedy at a school:

> Days like today remind us that the need for safe schools move across age ranges, across racial and socio-economic boundaries, across geographic boundaries. They remind us that our schools, as much as we wish them to be safe havens from the dangers of the world, too often are not. And they remind us of how much more work we have left to do. Moments like this are when you hug your children—your students and your "real" children—and hope for a better world, one where this kind of tragedy and violence doesn't have to happen—not in our schools, not anywhere.[59]

Primary Source Quotes*

Can School Violence Be Stopped?

❝ **The media hysteria encouraged people who run schools to do crazy things, like spend thousands of dollars on security cameras, and hire police officers to guard the doors. . . . Though school violence was down, studies show kids were more scared.** ❞

—John Stossel, "The School Violence Myth," ABC News.com, April 18, 2007. http://abcnews.go.com.

Stossel is an author, reporter, and coanchor of the TV news program *20/20*.

❝ **If we can place cameras in communities to monitor drug corners and dangerous offenders, then we can place them inside and outside of the schools for the safety of our students.** ❞

—Jody Weis, quoted in Fran Spielman, "City Linking School Security Cameras to Cops, 911 Center," *Chicago Sun-Times*, March 7, 2008. www.suntimes.com.

Weis, a former FBI agent, is the police superintendent in Chicago.

Bracketed quotes indicate conflicting positions.

* Editor's Note: While the definition of a primary source can be narrowly or broadly defined, for the purposes of Compact Research, a primary source consists of: 1) results of original research presented by an organization or researcher; 2) eyewitness accounts of events, personal experience, or work experience; 3) first-person editorials offering pundits' opinions; 4) government officials presenting political plans and/or policies; 5) representatives of organizations presenting testimony or policy.

Primary Source Quotes

66 Probably the most important thing to know about school shootings is that they can be prevented. A government study has found that in 81% of school shootings, the attackers tell other students about their plans. 99

—Daniel Gross, quoted in Colleen Coffey, "School Violence Prevention Expert Urges Action After Series of Five School Shootings in One Week," PAX, February 15, 2008.

Gross, whose younger brother was critically wounded in a shooting rampage, is the founder of the antiviolence organization PAX.

66 There's no surefire way of knowing who the next school shooter is going to be. 99

—Tom Rollins, quoted in Norman Draper, "School Violence Is Subject That Has No Simple Answers," *Minneapolis Star Tribune*, October 10, 2006. www.startribune.com.

Rollins's son Aaron was killed in 2003 by a fellow student at Rocori High School in Cold Spring, Minnesota.

66 Decreasing violence in schools requires a joint commitment from the school, the students, the parents, and the community. 99

—Jodi Dworkin, "What If the Next Shooting Is at My School?" *Teen Talk*, University of Minnesota Extension Service. www.extension.umn.edu.

Dworkin is an assistant professor in the Department of Family Social Science and the University of Minnesota Extension Service.

66 How does one protect oneself from someone whose goal is to take the lives of others even at the cost of his own? Sadly, the answer is that it is virtually impossible to stop such a person. 99

—John F. McManus, "Thoughts About Virginia Tech," *New American*, May 14, 2007.

McManus is president of the John Birch Society, an organization that is dedicated to preserving the freedoms granted by the U.S. Constitution.

66 Some people who do not like the idea of teachers being armed to protect students simply get indignant, or
declare that armed teachers are inconsistent with a
learning environment. I suggest that dead students—
and the traumatic aftermath of a school attack—are far
more inconsistent with a learning environment than
is a math teacher having a concealed handgun. 99

—Dave Kopel, "The Resistance," *National Review Online*, October 10, 2006. http://article.nationalreview.com.

Kopel is the research director at the Independence Institute.

66 We have problems in our schools, but not to the point
where we need to arm our teachers and principals. 99

—Pete Pochowski, quoted in Erin Richards, "Legislator Suggests Arming Teachers," *Milwaukee Journal Sentinel*,
October 4, 2006. www.jsonline.com.

Pochowski is the director of school safety for Milwaukee Public Schools.

66 Sometimes when people are intent on harming others,
the only reasonable response you could have is to con-
front them with firepower to stop them. 99

—Frank Lasee, quoted in Erin Richards, "Legislator Suggests Arming Teachers," *Milwaukee Journal Sentinel*, October 4,
2006. www.jsonline.com.

Lasee is a state assemblyman in Wisconsin.

66 I would be opposed to any guns in school, period. No
matter where I would put a gun in a classroom, a class
full of little people would find it. And if it were locked
up safely, there would be no chance to get it. 99

—Kim Campbell, quoted in CBS News.com, "After Shootings, Some Teachers Get Guns," October 16, 2006.
www.cbsnews.com.

Campbell is the president of the Utah Education Association.

66 While human nature causes us to focus our attention on our most horrific attacks, these are only representative of one type of campus weapons assault. Weapons reduction strategies must address the wide variety of violence that can occur. **99**

—Michael Dorn and Chris Dorn, "Proven Tactics to Prevent Campus Weapons Assaults," *College Planning & Management*, June 2007.

Dorn and Dorn are internationally recognized experts on weapons reductions strategies for campuses.

66 No single measure or combination of measures can ensure that deranged individuals are prevented in every instance from shooting up a crowded classroom. . . . But neither the absence of a perfect solution nor opposition from the powerful gun lobby is an excuse to do nothing—not when some 30 people are killed with guns every day in America. **99**

—*New York Times*, "Gun Crazy," editorial, March 1, 2008.

The *New York Times* editorial staff advocates gun control measures to cut down on gun violence in America.

Facts and Illustrations

Can School Violence Be Stopped?

- More than 200 studies have shown that antibullying programs have **reduced** fighting and other school violence by as much as **50 percent**.

- Schools that have implemented violence prevention programs have recorded anywhere from a **15 to 50 percent** reduction rate in violent and aggressive behavior.

- In student surveys, more than **80 percent** said they would be more likely to report crimes, threats, or suspicious behavior if they could do so anonymously.

- According to the CDC, nearly **50 percent** of school-related homicide perpetrators gave some type of warning signal prior to committing their crimes.

- From 1999 to 2006, the number of public schools that controlled access during school hours rose from **74.6 percent to 84.9 percent**.

- The largest percentage of schools that reported taking disciplinary action during 2005–2006 did so **in response to a physical attack or fight**.

- From 1999 to 2006, schools that used security cameras to monitor school activity rose from **19.4 percent to 42.8 percent**.

State Regulation of Teachers Carrying Guns

Although the issue of guns on college campuses is highly controversial, more states are considering legislation that would allow teachers to be armed. Currently, Utah is the only state that allows students and professors to carry guns at all public colleges. In Colorado, students can carry guns on all college campuses except for the University of Colorado, Boulder. This map shows where legislation has passed, failed, or is pending as of April 2008.

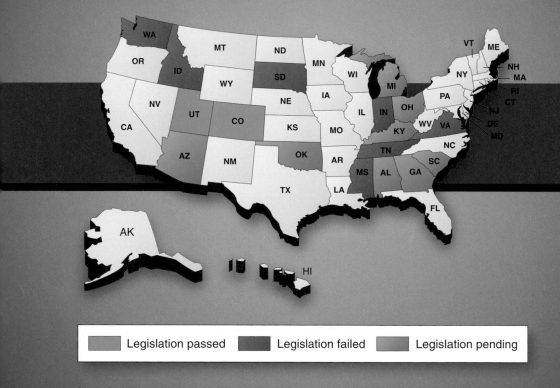

Legislation passed   Legislation failed   Legislation pending

Source: Brady Campaign, "Guns in Colleges and Schools?" 2008. www.bradycampaign.org.

- As of January 2008 the Speak Up program had received more than **20,000 calls** from students, which resulted in hundreds of weapons being confiscated and numerous threats being averted.

- During the 2006–2007 school year, nearly **6,000 incidents** were reported anonymously to the Talk About It service.

- Utah is the only state in the United States that allows students and professors to **carry guns at all public colleges**.

Top 10 Problems Facing Students

It is widely believed that many acts of school violence could be prevented if students were not reluctant to report suspicious activity, threats, and crimes when they hear about them. Anonymous communication services such as AnComm's "Talk About It®" are being used in growing numbers of schools as a way for young people to break the code of silence without fearing retaliation or feeling like snitches. During the 2006–2007 school year more than 50,000 students reported problems or threats in their schools. This chart shows the top-10 issues discussed.

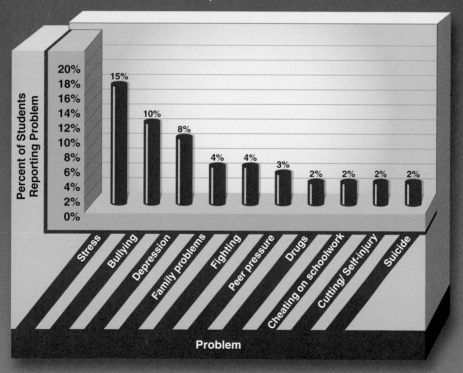

Source: "New Report Reveals Top Ten Problems Facing U.S. Students," AnComm News & Events, June 13, 2007. www.ancomm.com.

Can Zero Tolerance Policies Stop School Violence?

In an effort to curb violence, some schools have passed zero-tolerance policies that make most any infraction of school rules or behavior violations punishable with severe disciplinary measures. During February 2008, nearly 1,500 people responded to an About.com opinion poll titled *School Violence Poll for Parents*. This pie chart shows how they answered when asked the question,

"Should all schools adopt a zero-tolerance policy towards any type of violence?"

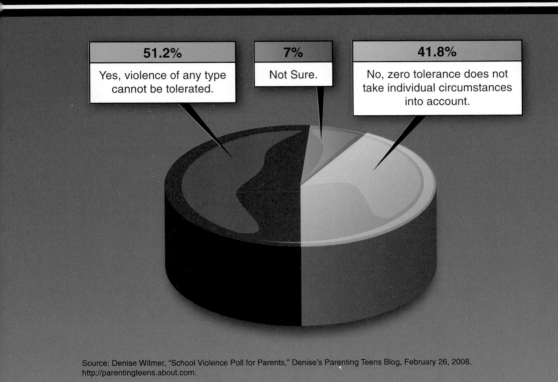

51.2%	7%	41.8%
Yes, violence of any type cannot be tolerated.	Not Sure.	No, zero tolerance does not take individual circumstances into account.

Source: Denise Witmer, "School Violence Poll for Parents," Denise's Parenting Teens Blog, February 26, 2008. http://parentingteens.about.com.

- According to April 2007 Congressional testimony, annual surveys of over 700 school-based police officers found that from school years 2001 to 2004, **84 to 89 percent** of crimes occurring in school were unreported to law enforcement.

Students' Feelings on Intruders' Access to School

Acts of school violence are usually committed by students—but not always. Sometimes intruders enter schools with the intent of inflicting harm on students and/or teachers, and no one stops them from getting inside. This concerns security experts and law enforcement, who insist that identifying people who are not supposed to be in schools is an essential element in violence prevention programs. Some schools have such practices in place, while others do not. During a November 2006 poll, 1,114 U.S. children and teenagers were asked about their schools' policies on intruders.

"Has someone at your school (for example a teacher, principal, or school administrator) spoken to you about what to do if an intruder or someone who does not belong in your school enters your school?"

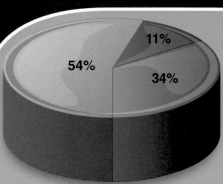

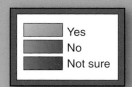

Yes
No
Not sure

"How likely is it that an intruder or someone who does not belong in your school could enter your school?"

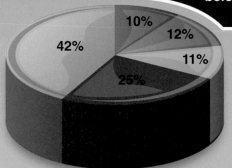

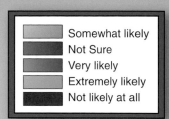

Somewhat likely
Not Sure
Very likely
Extremely likely
Not likely at all

Note: Percentages may not add up to 100 percent due to rounding.

Source: Harris Interactive, "Intruders in Our Public Schools: Two-Thirds of Youth and Three-Quarters of Parents Find It Likely That an Intruder Could Enter a School," December 12, 2006.

Key People and Advocacy Groups

Vincent Bove: Bove is a crime prevention expert who represents the families of victims of the Virginia Tech shooting.

Seung-Hui Cho: Cho was the gunman who committed the April 2007 shootings at Virginia Tech University, the deadliest school shooting that has ever occurred in the United States.

Dewey Cornell: Cornell is a forensic clinical psychologist and director of the Virginia Youth Violence Project at the University of Virginia.

Daniel Gross: After his younger brother was critically wounded in a New York City shooting, Gross founded the antiviolence group PAX and is a leading spokesperson on the gun violence issue.

Eric Harris and Dylan Klebold: Both seniors at Columbine High School in Littleton, Colorado, Harris and Klebold perpetrated the April 1999 shooting that left 14 students and a teacher dead and injured more than 20 others.

Patrick Ireland: After being shot and seriously wounded in the Columbine shooting, Ireland was rescued when he toppled out of a school window and became known throughout the media as the "boy in the window."

Stephen P. Kazmierczak: In what became known as the Valentine's Day school massacre, Kazmierczak killed five students and himself in a shooting rampage at Northern Illinois University on February 14, 2008.

Andrew Kehoe: In one of the worst school massacres in American history, Kehoe bombed a schoolhouse in Bath, Michigan in 1927, killing 45 people, including 38 children, and injuring more than 50 others.

Charles Carl Roberts: Roberts, a milk truck driver, killed five young girls and seriously wounded five other girls during an October 2006 shooting at an Amish schoolhouse in Nickel Mines, Pennsylvania.

Jason Della Rocca: As executive director of the International Game Developers Association (IGDA), Della Rocca is outspoken about his belief that video games are not responsible for real-life violence.

Regina Rohde: Rohde is a survivor of the Columbine High School shooting and was also a student at Virginia Tech when the April 2007 shooting occurred.

Dave Sanders: A favorite teacher at Columbine High School, Sanders died from wounds sustained in the 1999 shooting and was later hailed as a hero for helping so many students escape to safety before he was shot.

Jack Thompson: Thompson is a Florida attorney who is a fervent, outspoken critic of violent video games, saying that they contribute to real-life acts of violence.

Chronology

1927
Andrew Kehoe sets off a massive explosion at a schoolhouse in the rural village of Bath, Michigan, killing 38 children and 7 adults (including himself) and injuring more than 50 others.

1976
Edward Charles Allaway, a former custodian at California State University, Fullerton, uses a .22 caliber rifle to shoot 9 people in the school's library; 7 of the victims die.

1997
Michael Carneal, a 14-year-old student at Heath High School in West Paducah, Kentucky, opens fire on a youth prayer group at the school, killing 3 people and wounding 5 others.

1996
Armed with 4 handguns, unemployed store owner Thomas Hamilton storms into the gymnasium at Dunblane Primary School in central Scotland and starts shooting, killing 16 children and one teacher and wounding 10 others.

1925   **1950**   **1975**

1958
A deadly fire breaks out in Our Lady of the Angels school in Chicago, claiming the lives of 92 children and 3 nuns and injuring more than 100 others. A former student confesses to setting the fire at the school, but a judge does not hold him accountable, and the cause is officially listed as undetermined.

1989
Marc Lépine goes on a shooting rampage at L'École Polytechnique in Montreal, Quebec, Canada, killing 13 female students and an employee of the college and wounding 13 others.

1998
Dressed in camouflage fatigues and carrying handguns and rifles, 13-year-old Mitchell Johnson and 11-year-old Andrew Golden trigger a fire alarm at Westside Middle School near Jonesboro, Arkansas, and then start firing when students and teachers are leaving the school. After the shooting, 4 students and a teacher are dead, and 9 students and a teacher are wounded.

1966
Architectural engineering student and former U.S. Marine Charles Whitman barricades himself on the observation deck of the Main Building at the University of Texas at Austin and begins shooting with a sniper rifle. An hour and a half later, 16 people are dead, 31 others are wounded, and Whitman is killed by police.

2007

In the deadliest school shooting in U.S. history, Seung-Hui Cho goes on a violent rampage at Virginia Polytechnic Institute and State University in Blacksburg, Virginia, killing 27 students and 5 faculty members and wounding more than 24 others.

Pekka-Eric Auvinené shoots and kills 7 students and the principal at Jokela High School in Tuusula, Finland, and wounds 12 others, just hours after he posts a video on YouTube predicting a massacre.

1999

Wearing long black trench coats to conceal their weapons, Columbine High School seniors Eric Harris and Dylan Klebold go on a shooting rampage at the school, killing 12 students and a teacher and wounding 24 others.

2005

Jeffrey Weise, a 16-year-old student, opens fire at Red Lake High School at the Red Lake Band of Chippewa's reservation in Minnesota, leaving five students, a teacher, and a security guard dead.

2000

2005

2002

Former student Robert Steinhäeuser, heavily armed and wearing a mask, goes on a shooting spree at Johann Gutenberg Gymnasium in Erfurt, Germany, killing 12 teachers, one administrator, 2 students, and a police officer.

2004

Chechen militants storm School No. 1 in Beslan, Russia, taking more than 1,100 students and teachers hostage. The hostages are held in the gymnasium for 3 days, and then explosions rock the school, sending terrified hostages streaming outside. More than 300 people are killed, including 156 children, and over 700 others are wounded.

2008

Armed with a shotgun and 3 handguns, Stephen Kazmierczak walks onto the stage at a lecture hall at Northern Illinois University and begins firing at the audience, killing five people and wounding 16 others. Then, still standing on the stage, he shoots himself to death.

2006

Charles Carl Roberts walks into an Amish schoolhouse in Nickel Mines, Pennsylvania, and shoots 10 young girls execution-style; five of the girls die, and the others are seriously wounded.

President George W. Bush hosts the country's first Conference on School Safety in Chevy Chase, Maryland.

Related Organizations

AnComm, Inc.

9 Industrial Park Dr., Suite 106

Oxford, MS 38655

phone (toll-free): (866) 926-2666 • fax: (662) 281-9917

e-mail: info@ancomm.com • Web site: www.ancomm.com

AnComm's mission is to empower students to share what they know or what they hear before violence strikes at their school. The organization's Talk About It program provides a way for young people to use the Internet anonymously to report threats, instances of bullying, or crime. The Web site offers a white paper about school safety, a short Web seminar called "Breaking the Code of Silence," news releases, and articles.

Center for the Prevention of School Violence

4112 Pleasant Valley Rd., Suite 214

Raleigh, NC 27612

phone (toll-free): (800) 299-6054 • fax: (919) 715-1208

Web site: www.ncdjjdp.org

The Center for the Prevention of School Violence serves as a resource center and think tank for efforts that promote safer schools and foster positive youth development. The Web site offers school violence statistics, research bulletins, articles for parents and students, and links to other resources.

Centers for Disease Control and Prevention (CDC)

600 Clifton Rd.

Atlanta, GA 30333

phone: (404) 498-1515 • toll-free: (800) 311-3435

e-mail: info@cdc.gov • Web site: www.cdc.gov

The CDC is part of the U.S. Department of Health and Human Services, and its mission is to promote health and quality of life by preventing and controlling disease, injuries, and disabilities. The Web site has a special "School Violence" section that offers statistics, tips on coping with the aftermath of a tragedy, and a *Coping with Traumatic Stress* podcast.

National Alliance for Safe Schools

PO Box 335

Slanesville, WV 25444-0335

phone: (304) 496-8100 • fax: (304) 496-8105

e-mail: nass@frontier.net • Web site: www.safeschools.org

The National Alliance for Safe Schools offers training, school security assessments, and technical assistance for school districts, educational organizations, law enforcement, and parent groups. The Web site is informative about the organization's history, mission, and current work.

National Association of School Safety and Law Enforcement Officers (NASSLEO)

PO Box 210079

Milwaukee, WI 53221

phone: (315) 529-4858 • fax: (877) 282-4860

e-mail: nassleo@nassleo.org • Web site: www.nassleo.org

An organization composed of educators and law enforcement and security officers, NASSLEO is dedicated to keeping schools safe by providing professional information, training, and miscellaneous resources to school districts and law enforcement agencies across the United States and Canada. Its Web site offers a scholarship program that provides financial assistance to students who have chosen to further their education and are considering a career in school security and/or law enforcement.

National Center for Victims of Crime

2000 M St. NW, Suite 480

Washington, DC 20036

phone: (202) 467-8700 • fax: (202) 467-8701

e-mail: webmaster@ ncvc.org • Web site: www.ncvc.org

The National Center for Victims of Crime is a leading resource and advocacy organization for crime victims and those who serve them. It provides direct services to victims of crime throughout the United States and delivers training and technical assistance to victim service groups, counselors, attorneys, and other professionals who work with crime victims. Its Web site features materials especially for teen crime victims, as well as a resource library with statistics and other materials.

National Crime Prevention Council

345 Crystal Dr., Suite 500

Arlington, VA 22202-4801

phone: (202) 466-6272 • fax: (202) 296-1356

Web site: www.ncpc.org

The National Crime Prevention Council produces tools and crime prevention strategies that help keep people and communities safe. It is most famous for its McGruff the Crime Dog logo. Its Web site offers numerous publications on a variety of issues, news releases, pamphlets, and newsletters.

National Education Association (NEA)

1201 16th St. NW

Washington, DC 20036-3290

phone: (202) 833-4000 • fax: (202) 822-7974

e-mail: info@nea.org • Web site: www.nea.org

The NEA is committed to advancing the cause of public education in the United States and has more than 3 million members who work at every level of education, from preschool to university graduate programs. Its Web site's "Preventing School Violence" section offers a variety of publications on topics such as bullying in schools, strategies to stop school violence, and a report by the Secret Service.

National School Safety and Security Services

Cleveland, OH 44111

phone: (216) 251-3067, ext. *03

Web site: www.schoolsecurity.org

The National School Safety and Security Services is a consulting firm that provides school security assessments, school safety and school emergency/crisis planning, and other safety consulting services for K–12 schools. Its Web site provides a newsletter, legislative testimonies, articles about gangs and other topics, and a wealth of information about school crime and crime reporting.

National School Safety Center

141 Duesenberg Dr., Suite 11

Westlake Village, CA 91362

phone: (805) 373-9977 • fax: (805) 373-9277

Web site: www.schoolsafety.us

The National School Safety Center serves as an advocate for safe schools worldwide and acts as a catalyst for the prevention of school crime and violence by providing quality resources, consultation, and training services. A wide variety of information is available on its Web site, such as school crime and violence statistics, a publication on school-related violent deaths, articles on bullying, and its *Creating Safe Schools* pamphlet.

PAX/Real Solutions to Gun Violence

100 Wall St., 2nd Fl.

New York, NY 10005

phone: (212) 269-5100 • toll-free: (800) 983-4275

toll-free phone for reporting a weapon threat at school:

(866) SPEAK-UP (866-773-2587)

fax: (212) 269-5109

e-mail: info@paxusa.org • Web site: www.paxusa.org

PAX is a nonprofit organization whose mission is to end gun violence against children and families, and its national ASK and Speak Up programs are designed to expand public awareness of gun violence. Its Web site offers real-life stories, statistics, news releases, and various articles.

Students Against Violence Everywhere (SAVE)

322 Chapanoke Rd., Suite 110

Raleigh, NC 27603

phone: (919) 661-7800 • toll-free: (866) 343-SAVE

fax: (919) 661-7777

e-mail: info@nationalsave.org • Web site: www.nationalsave.org

SAVE is a student-initiated organization that strives to decrease the potential for school violence by promoting student involvement, education, and service opportunities in order to make learning environments safer for young people. Its Web site offers the *SAVE eSource* newsletter, school violence facts and figures, news releases, and a variety of resources just for teens.

For Further Research

Books

Lucinda Almond, *School Violence*. Detroit: Greenhaven, 2007.

Scott Barbour, *How Can School Violence Be Prevented?* Detroit: Greenhaven, 2004.

Brooks Brown, *No Easy Answers: The Truth Behind Death at Columbine*. New York: Lantern, 2002.

Dewey G. Cornell, *School Violence: Fears Versus Facts*. Mahwah, NJ: Lawrence Erlbaum Associates, 2006.

Susan C. Hunnicutt, *School Shootings*. Detroit: Greenhaven, 2006.

Tricia Jones and Randy Compton, *Kids Working It Out: Stories and Strategies for Making Peace in Our Schools*. San Francisco: Jossey-Bass, 2003.

Marjorie Lindholm and Peggy Lindholm, *A Columbine Survivor's Story*. Littleton, CO: Regenold, 2005.

Dennis Lines, *The Bullies: The Rationale of Bullying*. Philadelphia: Jessica Kingsley, 2008.

National Research Council, *Deadly Lessons: Understanding Lethal School Violence*. Washington, DC: National Academies Press, 2003.

Katherine S. Newman et al., *Rampage: The Social Roots of School Shootings*. New York: Basic Books, 2005.

Beth Nimmo and Darrell Scott, *Rachel's Tears: The Spiritual Journey of Columbine Martyr Rachel Scott*. Nashville, TN: Thomas Nelson, 2000.

Rick Phillips, John Linney, and Chris Pack, *Safe School Ambassadors: Harnessing Student Power to Stop Bullying and Violence*. San Francisco: Jossey-Bass, 2008.

Kathy Sexton-Radek, *Violence in Schools: Issues, Consequences, and Expressions*. Westport, CT: Praeger, 2004.

R. Murray Thomas, *Violence in America's Schools: Understanding, Prevention, and Responses*. Westport, CT: Praeger, 2006.

Periodicals

Stephanie Booth, "Why Your Campus Can Be a Danger Zone," *Cosmopolitan*, January 2008.

Tobias Buck, "Gunman Kills Eight in Attack on Jerusalem School," *Financial Times*, March 7, 2008.

Kevin Butler, "Tragic Lessons: Deadly School Violence Causes Districts to Take Stock and Revamp Security," *District Administration*, May 2007.

Benedict Carey, "Reports of Gunman's Use of Antidepressant Renew Debate over Side Effects," *New York Times*, February 19, 2008.

Rebecca Cathcart, "Boy's Killing, Labeled a Hate Crime, Stuns a Town," *New York Times*, February 23, 2008.

Gail Russell Chaddock, "How to Make US Schools Safer," *Christian Science Monitor*, October 12, 2006.

Eve Conant, "Class Conflicts," *Vogue*, September 2007.

Mensah M. Dean, "Schools: Violence, Crime Rises," *Philadelphia Daily News*, March 11, 2008.

Elizabeth Donald, "New Text 'E-lert' Emergency System Goes into Effect at SIUE: Poses an Issue for Teachers Who Ban Phones," *Belleville (IL) News-Democrat*, March 4, 2008.

Michael Dorn, "Play It Smart, Play It Safe," *School Planning and Management*, January 2007.

———, "Preventing School Weapons Assaults," *Doors & Hardware*, March 2008.

Marilyn Elias, "Before Tragedy Struck, Signs Were There," *USA Today*, February 20, 2008.

James Alan Fox and Jack Levin, "Perpetuating School Violence: How to Find New Ways to Keep Schools Safe," *District Administration*, May 2004.

Bill Hewitt, "Heartbreak in a Small Town," *People Weekly*, October 16, 2006.

———, "His Twisted, Tragic Path," *People Weekly*, September 17, 2007.

Brad Knickerbocker, "Should Teachers Be Allowed to Pack a Gun?" *Christian Science Monitor*, September 18, 2007.

Donna Leinwand, "States Work to Close Gun-Law Gap," *USA Today*, February 19, 2008.

Angus MacLeod, "Forty-five Exclusions per Hour as Violence Soars in Scottish Schools," *Times* (London), January 30, 2008.

Nick Martin, "Winnipeg Schools Use Beads to Battle Bullying," *Winnipeg Free Press*, March 3, 2008.

Bob Meadows, "This Is Only a Drill," *People Weekly*, June 18, 2007.

Kira Millage, "Students Take on Rachel's Challenge: Slain Columbine Teen Wanted to Spread Kindness," *Bellingham Herald*, February 10, 2008.

Geoff Mulvihill, "Teen Suspected of Plot Was Fixated on War," *Hackensack (NJ) Record*, March 7, 2008.

Andrew Murr, "Is Your Campus Safe?" *Newsweek*, August 2007.

Sara Neufeld, "Schools Strive to Stem Violence," *Baltimore Sun*, December 29, 2007.

Andrew Potter, "Colleges Can't Be More Like Airports? Why Not?" *Maclean's*, April 30, 2007.

Stacy A. Teicher, "How Students Can Break the 'Code of Silence,'" *Christian Science Monitor*, October 19, 2006.

Margaret Wente, "Expelled for Committing Assault with a Deadly Pen," *Globe and Mail* (Toronto), February 5, 2008.

Pat Wingert, "How to Prevent a Tragedy," *Newsweek*, January 7, 2008.

Internet Sources

Tony Burchyns, "Videotaped Brawls Put Schools in Pickle," *Contra Costa (CA) Times*, February 1, 2008. www.contracostatimes.com/ci_8139029.

Anne Carey et al., "Illinois Classroom Terror," *USA Today*, February 16, 2008. www.usatoday.com/news/nation/2008-02-16-shooting_N.htm.

Dewey Cornell, "School Violence: Assessing the Threat," *Washington Post*, April 17, 2007. www.washingtonpost.com.

Bill Dedman, "10 Myths About School Shootings," MSNBC, October 10, 2007. www.msnbc.msn.com.

Tamara Jones and Joshua Partlow, "Pa. Killer Had Prepared for Long Siege," *Washington Post,* October 4, 2006. www.washingtonpost.com.

James H. Noonan and Malissa C. Vavra, "Crime in Schools and Colleges: A Study of Offenders and Arrestees Reported via National Incident-Based Reporting System Data," October 2007. www.fbi.gov/ucr/schoolviolence/2007/schoolviolence.pdf.

Edith Starzyk, "Ominous Signs Hover over School Violence Statistics," *Metro*, Cleveland.com, January 27, 2008. http://blog.cleveland.com/metro/2008/01/ominous_signs_hover_over_schoo.html.

John Stossel, "The School Violence Myth," ABC News.com, April 18, 2007. http://abcnews.go.com/2020/story?id=3053333&page=1.

Peter Wilkinson, "Columbine, Five Years Later," *Salon*, April 20, 2004. http://dir.salon.com/story/mwt/feature/2004/04/20/columbine_anniversary.

Source Notes

Overview

1. Quoted in Court TV, "Schools Under Fire?" October 4, 2006. www.courttv.com.
2. Quoted in Bradley Campbell, "Beat Down," *Cleveland Scene*, February 20, 2008. www.clevescene.com.
3. Laurence Miller, "Practical Police Psychology," Police One, April 20, 2007. www.policeone.com.
4. Quoted in Katherine Tweed, "Mental Health and School Violence," Fox News.com, February 15, 2008. www.foxnews.com.
5. Quoted in Sara Neufeld, "Schools Try to Stem Violence," *Baltimore Sun*, December 29, 2007. www.baltimoresun.com.
6. Quoted in Greg Toppo, "Keeping School Violence at Bay," *USA Today*, June 27, 2004. www.usatoday.com.
7. Quoted in Winda Benedetti, "Were Video Games to Blame for Massacre?" MSNBC, April 20, 2007. www.msnbc.msn.com.
8. Quoted in Benedetti, "Were Video Games to Blame for Massacre?"
9. Quoted in Eric Pooley, "Portrait of a Deadly Bond," *Time*, May 10, 1999. www.time.com.
10. Quoted in Stephanie Booth, "Why Your Campus Can Be a Danger Zone," *Cosmopolitan*, January 2008, p. 123.
11. Quoted in Laura Hancock, "KBYU-FM Focuses on Effects of School Violence," *Deseret Morning News*, April 19, 2005. http://deseretnews.com.
12. Quoted in Andrew Johnson, "Impact of School Shootings Called Worse than That of War," *Pittsburgh Tribune-Review*, October 5, 2006. www.pittsburghlive.com.
13. Quoted in *The Early Show*, "After Shootings, Some Teachers Get Guns," CBS News.com, October 16, 2006. www.cbsnews.com.
14. Quoted in Court TV, "Schools Under Fire?"
15. Quoted in Gerri Hirshey, "Pushing Back at Bullying," *New York Times*, January 28, 2007. www.nytimes.com.

How Widespread Is School Violence?

16. Laura Standley, "Student Reacts to Northern Illinois Shooting," letter to the editor, *Temple News*, March 3, 2008. http://temple-news.com.
17. Quoted in Ted Gregory and David Elsner, "NIU Gunman Identified," *Chicago Tribune*, March 31, 2008. www.chicagotribune.com.
18. Quoted in Daryl Presgraves, "National Gun Violence Prevention Organization Demands Solutions After 8-Year-Old Boy Shoots 7-Year-Old Girl at Daycare," PAX, January 26, 2006. www.paxusa.org.
19. Quoted in Todd Zwillich, "CDC: School Homicides Are Rare," Web MD, January 17, 2008. www.webmd.com.
20. Laurence Miller, "School Violence: The Psychology of Youthful Mass Murder and What to Do About It," Police One, April 20, 2007. www.policeone.com.
21. Quoted in John E. Reid, "Confession Interview," OLA Fire Memorial. www.olafire.com.
22. Quoted in Dennis McMillan, "Bias-Related Harassment Plagues Public Schools," *San Francisco Bay Times*, November 1, 2007. www.sfbaytimes.com.

23. National School Safety and Security Services, "Why Is It Important for Schools to Report Crimes?" www.schoolsecurity.org.

24. Quoted in Neal McCluskey, "Violence in Public Schools: A Dirty Secret," The Heartland Institute, June 1, 2005. www.heartland.org.

25. Quoted in Shawn D. Lewis, "Teacher Recovers from Attack," *Detroit News*, March 26, 2008. www.detnews.com.

26. Quoted in Russ Bynum, "Cops: 3rd-Graders Plotted Teacher Attack," *Buffalo News*, April 2, 2008. www.buffalo news.com.

What Are the Causes of School Violence?

27. Miller, "School Violence."

28. Quoted in Bill Whitaker, "Remembering the Massacre 8 Years Ago," CBS News.com, April 20, 2007. www.cbsnews.com.

29. Quoted in Julie Jüttner, "Armed to the Teeth and Crying for Help," *Der Spiegel International*, November 21, 2006. www.spiegel.de.

30. Centers for Disease Control and Prevention, "New Technology and Youth Violence," December 3, 2007. www.cdc.gov.

31. Carly Weeks, "Many Blame Violence on Bad Parents," *Leader-Post*, June 2, 2007. www.canada.com.

32. Louise Last, "School Violence," *AllPsych Journal*, November 15, 2001. http://allpsych.com.

33. Quoted in CNN.com, "Columbine Shooters Documented Their Rage on Home Videos," December 14, 1999. http://archives.cnn.com.

34. Quoted in Fiona Morgan, "Learning from Littleton," *Salon*, April 27, 1999. www.salon.com.

35. Quoted in The Gun Source, "Owner of Web-Based Firearms Company That Sold to Virginia Tech and NIU Shooters Looks to Turn Tragedy into Platform to Improve Public Safety." www.thegunsource.com.

36. John E. Rosenthal, "Had Enough Gun Violence?" *Christian Science Monitor*, February 20, 2008. www.csmonitor.com.

37. Adele M. Brodkin, "In the Aftermath of Violence," *Junior Scholastic— Teacher's Edition*, October 30, 2006, p. T5.

38. Quoted in Norman Miller, "Prosecutor Outlines L-S Murder Suspect John Odgren's History of Violence," *MetroWest Daily News*, March 6, 2007. www.metrowestdailynews.com.

What Is the Aftermath of School Violence?

39. Quoted in Tillie Fong, "Déjà Vu for Survivor at Tech," *Rocky Mountain News*, April 19, 2007. www.rockymountainnews.com.

40. Quoted in Peter Wilkinson, "Columbine, Five Years Later," *Salon*, April 20, 2004. http://dir.salon.com.

41. Quoted in Whitaker, "Remembering the Massacre 8 Years Ago."

42. Quoted in Tom Beardon, "Survivors of Virginia Tech Shootings Face Long Road to Normalcy," *PBS, Online NewsHour*, April 25, 2007. www.pbs.org.

43. Quoted in Rex Bowman, "Va. Tech Families May Sue State," *Richmond Times-Dispatch*, March 26, 2008. www.inrich.com.

44. Quoted in Pierre Thomas et al., "Campus Shooting Highlights Legal Loophole," ABC News.com, February 19, 2008. http://abcnews.go.com.

45. Quoted in Fox News.com, "Wife of School Gunman Thanks Amish for Forgiveness," October 14, 2006. www.foxnews.com.

46. Quoted in CBS News.com, "Wounded Student: I Forgive Gunman," April

19, 2007. www.cbsnews.com.

47. Quoted in Kelli Kennedy, "Fla. Man Threatens Va. Tech–like Attack," Police One, April 4, 2008. www.police one.com.

48. Quoted in Jen Gerson, "Students, Community Traumatized, Experts Say," *Toronto Star*, May 23, 2007. www.thestar.com.

49. *Northern Star Online*, "Cole Hall Shooting: NIU Has Lost Members of Family," February 14, 2008. www. northernstar.info.

Can School Violence Be Stopped?

50. Michael Dorn, "Preventing School Weapons Assaults," *Doors & Hardware*, March 2008, p. 36.

51. Quoted in Toni Randolph, "Officials Say They Didn't Overreact to School Threat," Minnesota Public Radio, October 19, 2004. http://news.minne sota.publicradio.org.

52. Quoted in *Ashbury Park (NJ) Press*, "Threat 'Sent Chills Down My Spine,'"

February 22, 2008. www.app.com.

53. Quoted in PAX, "Real Stories from PAX Spokeskids," 2006. http://paxusa. org.

54. Quoted in Alan Shirk, "Haydenfilms, Olivet Boys and Girls Club Film 'Speak Up!' Video PSAs," Open Press, March 28, 2008. www.theopenpress. com.

55. Quoted in AnComm, "Testimonials." www.ancomm.com.

56. "You're All Gonna Die . . . Psych!" *Indiana Daily Student*, March 6, 2008. www.idsnews.com.

57. John F. McManus, "Thoughts About Virginia Tech," *New American*, May 14, 2007, pp. 44–45.

58. Dewey Cornell, "School Violence: Assessing the Threat," *Washington Post*, April 17, 2007. www.washington post.com.

59. Chris Lehmann, "Virginia Tech," Practical Theory, April 16, 2007. http://practicaltheory.org.

List of Illustrations

Index

About the Author

Peggy J. Parks holds a bachelor of science degree from Aquinas College in Grand Rapids, Michigan, where she graduated magna cum laude. She is an author who has written more than 70 nonfiction educational books for children and young adults, as well as self-published her own cookbook called *Welcome Home: Recipes, Memories, and Traditions from the Heart*. Parks lives in Muskegon, Michigan, a town that she says inspires her writing because of its location on the shores of Lake Michigan.